NOW I SEE!

What Others are Saying...

Talented author and speaker Janet Perez Eckles knows crushing disappointments. In *Now I See!*, her story assures us that even when the news is devastating, God is still at work. Janet illuminates a path through anxiety, sorrow, and sleeplessness to the Source of hope, strength, and purpose.

—PEGGY SUE WELLS
international speaker
bestselling author of 32 books including
The Ten Best Decisions a Single Mom Can Make and *The Patent*

Janet can see the invisible, and therefore God has done the impossible in her life. Her life story in *Now I See!* is riveting enough to feel as if you're living it alongside her. Her tragedies turned to triumph are uniquely adventurous, compelling, and heartwarming, inspiring incredible hope, all because of God's amazing grace. Janet's story has encouraged me to embark on a new, vibrant journey of experiencing God's greatest treasures in life. One I believe will lead me to my own victorious episodes and seasons.

— KELLY ANN BRADICICH
Founder and Executive Director,
Kelly-Ann Women's Ministry, Inc.
West Palm Beach, FL

I've been privileged to cross paths with Janet Perez Eckles professionally and personally for almost twenty years now. I've witnessed this "blind *chica* from Bolivia" fearlessly hopping planes alone across countless time zones to share her message of God's amazing grace. Seen her retain faith in God's goodness despite losing her son to a killer. Having spent years in Bolivia, I can testify that her incredible childhood experiences are not apocryphal. *Now I See!* brings alive Janet's astonishing life journey from physical blindness to joyous spiritual vision that blesses all she meets. I cannot recommend this book enough for any reader yearning in this world filled with darkness, pain, and despair to know God's love, healing, and redemption."

— JEANETTE WINDLE
investigative journalist
author of *All Saints*, *CrossFire*, and
*Forgiven: The Amish School Shooting,
a Mother's Love, and a Story of Remarkable Grace*

Now I See! is an honest account of pain and healing, sorrow and joy as Janet Perez Eckles shares her journey from growing up in Bolivia's poverty to a new life in America that brought blindness, betrayal, and death. With God's Word alive in her and the Holy Spirit as her companion, Janet has picked up her white cane of courage to communicate her message across the world in conferences, on television, and by radio, discovering in the process that pain, anguish, and devastation cross all borders, languages, and ethnicities. In these pages, you will discover how God restores those who call on Him, heals those who believe, and turns all things to good for those who truly love Him. I am proud to call Janet my friend, and I urge you to read this amazing book and share it with your family and friends.

— CHUCK GRAHAM
author, *Take the Stand* and *A Year of Encouragement*
Founder and Executive Director,
Ciloa International Ministries
Lawrenceville, GA

Now I See! is an amazing must-read that left me completely inspired by the Holy Spirit. I simply couldn't put it down. As I lived every moment through Janet's incredible journey, I cried, laughed, rejoiced, and marveled at every turn. Her zest for life in the midst of the darkest circumstances made me realize there is always a better way when we keep our focus on the Lord. Janet taught me resourcefulness as hers is beyond compare. I saw how God collected all the broken pieces of her life, placed them into a treasure box, and tied it with the ribbon of His love.

— KAREN FAITH HELLER
President, *Way Cool Angels, Inc.*
Addison, TX

If blinded eyes are truly opened, then it is your eyes that will be opened as you read Janet's compelling journey through her very real struggles with blindness. Your heart will be warmed by the story she tells of living with the ability to see things others cannot.

— WADE MUMM, PH.D.
lead pastor, *Greenway Church*
Orlando, FL

NOW I SEE!

How God's Amazing Grace Turned Betrayal, Blindness, and Heartache to Shining Joy

Janet Perez Eckles

Copyright © 2023 Janet Perez Eckles

ISBN (paperback) 979-8-9876437-0-9
ISBN (e-book) 979-8-9876437-1-6

Published by JC Empowerment Ministries, Orlando FL
Edited by Jeanette Windle (www.jeanettewindle.com)
Cover by Swapan Das (Bigpoints) (www.99designs.com)
Book and Ebook interior design and format created by EBook Listing Services (www.ebooklistingservices.com)
Visit the author at www.janetperezeckles.com.

Publisher's Cataloging-in-Publication Data
Names: Eckles, Janet Perez, author.
Title: Now I see : how God's amazing grace turned betrayal , blindness , and heartache to shining joy / by Janet Perez Eckles.
Description: Orlando, FL: JC Empowerment Ministries, 2023.
Identifiers: LCCN: 2023901179 | ISBN: 979-8-9876437-0-9 (print) | 979-8-9876437-1-6 ebook
Subjects: LCSH Eckles, Janet Perez. | Bolivian Americans--Biography. | Blind--Biography. | Self-actualization (Psychology) | Christian biography. | BISAC BIOGRAPHY & AUTOBIOGRAPHY / People with Disabilities | HEALTH & FITNESS / Vision | RELIGION / Christian Living / Inspirational | RELIGION / Christian Living / Personal Memoirs
Classification: LCC BR1725 .E35 2023 | DDC 270.092--dc23

Dedication

Gratitude dances in my heart as I dedicate not only this book but my life to **Jesus Christ**, who revolutionized my life and opened my spiritual eyes. When I tap my fingers on my computer keyboard, I hear my screen reader speak what I type. That's precisely how I navigate through my days in physical darkness—following God's guidance to something better, sweeter, and powerfully beautiful.

I dedicate my book as well to my **precious family**. While as author and speaker I still use the surname Perez Eckles, God brought into my life a wonderful godly man who made me Mrs. Dale Settles on December 1, 2019. My dearest friend, supporter, and companion, **Dale** has made my life richer with his love.

I thank God for other dear family members now looking down from heaven. My dad **Ito**, always an example of tenacity and courage. My mom **Ita**, whose wisdom, joy, and unconditional love nourished me, comforted me in painful moments, and encouraged me to follow Jesus and serve others above myself. And my youngest son **Joe**, who has now lived in the glory of heaven for twenty years.

Also family still close at hand. My brother **Ed** and his wife **Lois**. My two older sons **Jason** and **Jeffrey**. Their beautiful wives

Rachel and Krystal. And my precious grandchildren to date, Alyssa, Kamden, and Eliana. What a privilege to have them witness their blind Nana seeing life through the beauty of Christ's love. It is to each that I present this book, thanking God for the privilege of stringing words together to express His almighty power at work.

Table of Contents

Acknowledgements

As I look back over the pages of my life, so many people have cheered me on, offered encouragement, supported me through dark valleys, and helped me reach heights I never could have on my own. The list of these dear friends is far longer than can be enumerated here. But I would like to express a special thanks and appreciation to a few God has used in very special ways, including the writing of this book.

To **Cindi Lynch**, who has been the pillar of JC Empowerment Ministries. God didn't restore my physical sight but did something better. He brought Cindi to show me through her wisdom, dedication to God, diligence, and giving heart what a true servant of God looks like.

To **Sandy Meystedt**, whom God used to give me the courage to keep going.

To **Karen Faith Heller**, whose sweet demeanor always gives me reason to smile.

To **Patty Gomez**, whose counsel and wise words have always lifted me up.

To **Kelly Ann Bradicich**, whose support and words of encouragement are treasures to me.

To **Sandy and Bob Mahone**, whose friendship through the years has been a precious gift.

To **Pastor Wade Mumm**, whose consistent spiritual leadership has enriched my life and fueled my ministry.

To **Jeanette Windle**, whose editorial skills gave the final polish to this book. I have relished your constant encouragement and assistance as you became my eyes while we navigated through many author and writer conferences together over the years.

And to **you, my dear reader**, for investing your time in these pages. The prayers covering this project have included praying for you so that your own eyes may be opened to see the power of God's amazing grace.

FOREWORD
by Jason Noble

We are all just one phone call away from our life turning upside-down. What do we do when we get that call? Do we fall apart in fear or rise up in faith?

The book you are about to read will change your life and your perspective about how to navigate through disappointment, tragedy, and any other dark valley you face. It's a captivating story of how one woman overcame tremendous obstacles and trauma because of her perseverance and deep faith in God. Despite all she has gone through, Janet Perez Eckles is one of the most joyful people you will ever meet. The Bible tells us that the joy of the Lord is our strength (Nehemiah 8:10). It was in her darkest moments that Janet chose joy, and this joy would become her strength. In these pages, she illustrates how that strength can carry us through even unthinkable tragedy and sorrow.

Though Janet is physically blind, I am amazed at her ability to *see*. She can definitely see more than most people I know. In telling her story, Janet gives us great examples of how to *see* in the spiritual realm so that we may live victoriously. We simply cannot afford to be spiritually blind. As you read these pages with *ears to hear* and *eyes to see*, God will give you great insight into your own situation. You'll discover how to use God's filter to truly see your own challenges the way God sees them.

One commonly misunderstood scripture is Romans 8:28, which tells us "*And we know that God causes everything to work together for the good of those who love God and are called according to his purpose for them.*" (NLT)

It's important to notice what this scripture does not say. It doesn't claim that all things are good. Some things are bad, painful, and difficult. But if we love God, He takes all the bad and works them together for our good and His ultimate purpose. We see this truth play out in Janet's book again and again as God took terrible situations in her life and worked them for good.

Too often when we face suffering or fall into dark valleys, we want to know *why*. Since we may never know the *why*, we need instead to ask what. God, *what* do you want me to do with this situation? I believe the enemy of our soul wants us to ask the *why* question so he can convince us that God is not good. Janet didn't dwell on *why* these things happened in her life. Instead, she focused on the *what*. She poured her life into asking, "God, *what* do you want me to do with what I'm facing right now?"

In so doing, her own difficulties and tragedies have become a vivid illustration to help you and me walk through unthinkable challenges in our own lives. I am so excited for you to journey with Janet through this book and her story. You will be blessed in amazing ways and find yourself more prepared if the day should come when a single phone call or other unanticipated trauma turns your world upside-down. I pray you allow this book to stir your heart so you will *see* beyond the circumstance and transform your life into a triumphant journey.

Jason Noble

original true-life pastor featured in Twentieth Century Fox movie *Breakthrough* and publicist for Kingdom Story movie *Jesus Revolution*

lead pastor. *My Hope City Church*, White City, OR

INTRODUCTION

S ome say I should be stuck in the mud of misery. I'm not. Instead, I'm dancing on the stage of victory. But for this Bolivian *chica*, that journey hasn't been easy. In fact, it's been ugly and painful. I lost my sight at thirty. My youngest son was murdered, the man responsible acquitted. Then with no warning, my husband of forty-two years said *adios* and divorced me.

Each of the above episodes shoved me into a dungeon of devastation. Perhaps similar to one you might be in right now. Thankfully, God didn't leave me in the dungeon. Instead, He used my lowest points of devastation to guide me along a path to healing, redemption, and transformation. A path He invites you to take as well. That's why I am writing this book—so that you may join me on my journey. As you do, you might find God's treasures that will shine in the stages of your own life.

With your permission, then, may I come alongside you, dear friend? Let's begin by clearing the misconception that I'm the author and you are the reader. Not at all. We're friends already. If you have this book on your screen or in your hands, our bonding has begun. I'm here for you and with you.

Maybe at this moment you are sitting on the floor with the pieces of your broken heart strewn around you. Turmoil has turned your world upside down, and the flood of tears won't stop. Answers, healing, solutions, and change are nowhere to be found in the ugly chaos and dark fog of despair.

How do I know? Because I've been on that same floor of anguish where desperation was about to eat me for lunch. I didn't know what day it was, whether there was rain or sunshine outside, and I didn't even care. Fear and anguish became the intruders who refused to leave.

If you've been there, I wonder if your pain happened suddenly like mine. Did your distress tear at your every fiber and wound you beyond endurance? Or maybe it was a more gradual buildup of hurt and grief.

No matter what the answer, let me reassure you that God is right here with you as He was with me. He is whispering the dawning of freedom for you. But before we begin our journey together, let's take a moment to consider three steps: the present, God's power, and the path.

THE PRESENT

There is nothing we can do to change the ugliness of this world. There's no way we can turn the clock back before COVID-19. Or undo the virus that has infected our lives with heartache and grief. There's no way for us to resolve the hurt that pierced us yesterday or decades ago. We can't wipe the darkness away or make all beautiful again.

Unless...

GOD'S POWER

Unless we tap into God's power. His power is supernatural, ever-present, and majestic enough to demolish opposition, bring down walls of sorrow, and dismantle the devil's lies.

God's power is always at work. As He fights our battles, His Word is the sword that will slice the enemy to pieces. And let me add a daring truth. Through Christ Jesus, God will hand us victory on the platter of His love.

How can we be sure? Because He has done that very thing before. In biblical times. In recent times. In the depths of remote jungles. In the midst of crowded apartment buildings and in luxurious homes. God's power has been showcased in all places and nations.

And how will He display that same power in the privacy of your pain? The answer is in the path.

THE PATH

Together, you and I will start our journey along the path that takes us from the pitiful to the powerful. I could cite tons of Scripture, craft a stern sermon, or write lines of admonition. Instead, I will show you. The words in this book invite you into the bedroom of my heart. There you'll peek at the private rooms of my journey beginning with my days as a little girl in Bolivia whom God was preparing, perhaps to have me taste adversity at an early age.

You'll be the judge as you turn these pages, and you'll see how God's hand brings His promises alive. Not so much for my benefit but for yours. So that you may see how the God of the universe watches the details of our pain. How He collects our tears in a bottle. How He hears our sobs, sees our anguish, and knows yesterday's regrets. He knows the shame we keep zipped up in the secret compartment of our heart. And He's so aware of the loneliness, insecurities, and worry that whisper in the silence of our nights. The journey will be surprising yet exciting. Each turn will take you higher, bring you closer, and show you greater things.

Are you ready? Then here's a tissue. Wipe away that last tear, and let's hop on the ride. This is my story, but the message of God's amazing and radiant grace is yours. You'll read about trauma, betrayal, injustice, and grief. But you'll also see how God's power is alive and active as it heals, soothes, and brings joy unspeakable inside a guaranteed victory that's sweetly glorious.

CHAPTER ONE
REVOLUTION!

Do not be afraid. Stand firm and you will see the deliverance the
Lord will bring you today... The Lord will fight for you; you need
only to be still.

—Exodus 14:13

The afternoon sun shone bright in a cloudless blue sky as my
six-year-old brother and I played on our back patio, running up
and down the different levels of an overgrown garden. Two years
younger than me, Ed always found ways to torment his big sister.
Dangling a long worm between his fingers, he chased me around
the patio, calling out, "Hey, it's dead! It won't hurt you!"

In contrast, the majestic scenery of La Paz, Bolivia, where my
family lived, was very much alive all around us. A bowl-like
depression nestled into South America's Andes Mountains, La Paz
is the highest capital city in the world at well over twelve thousand
feet above sea level.

But thousands of feet higher, the glistening white glacier fields of Mount Illimani paint a majestic panorama. They provide a glorious background for the condors that soar overhead on wings that can span ten feet. Far below, indigenous Quechua and Aymara women herd flocks of sheep, llamas, and alpaca.

Down in the basin, La Paz's two million residents are spread out very much according to wealth and class. At the lower levels where a river waters green parklands, prosperous neighborhoods of comfortable whitewashed mansions and high rises cater to the wealthier classes. Poorer homes of mud brick climb the parched, steep sides of the basin, growing smaller and shabbier the higher they climb. The modest stucco home my parents, brother, and I shared with my paternal grandparents was partway up the mountainside near a military base.

On this particular afternoon in 1960 when I was eight years old, I was doing my best to ignore my younger brother since at that time we were the worst of enemies. Suddenly I heard a familiar but frightening sound. Ed and I both froze in place. The roar of fighter planes taking off from the nearby military base along with the *rat-tat-tat* of machine gun fire meant only one thing. Another revolution! Armed changes of government had become so common in recent decades it was joked that revolution rather than soccer was Bolivia's national sport.

Managing to unfreeze, Ed and I raced toward the back door of the house. My grandmother, or Abuelita as we called her (meaning "dear grandma"), stood in the doorway. Salt-and-pepper hair pulled back in a bun framed her wrinkled face. She wore a sweater she'd knitted herself and a white lace-edged apron over her black wool skirt. Her hands motioned with urgency. "Quickly, both of you! Get inside!"

The flight path for the fighter planes went right over our house. As another plane zoomed even closer overhead, every window rattled, protesting the intrusion. Ed and I ran to Abuelita. My heart thudded in my chest as I hugged her tight with trembling arms and pressed my face against her skirt. Holding our hands, she hurried Ed and me into her bedroom.

More fighter planes roared overhead like furious lions ready to snatch us. Ed and I pressed our hands to our ears as the three of us scrambled into a closet. I looked up at Abuelita. A lump in my throat hurt as I held back my tears. If I allowed them to flow, her worry for me would add to her nervousness. "When will it be over?"

"Soon. We'll be okay," Abuelita whispered, kissing the top of my head.

Hugging Ed and me tighter, Abuelita began reciting prayers aloud, but the intermittent noise outside drowned them out. My worried thoughts turned to my mom. How would she get home safely from work? Streets jammed with angry protestors would halt all bus service. That meant a forty-five minute climb from her job at the university library up the steep mountain dirt lanes to our home. Her trek would take much longer if she was forced to slip into the closest building for shelter from riots or gunfire.

At least my father should be safe. Days prior, he had traveled for work to another city. We assumed he'd have heard about this new revolution in the capital city through radio broadcasts. But there was no way to know until his return since a phone wasn't a luxury our family could afford.

Janet outside her home in La Paz.

The fighter planes overhead finally stopped, and we were able to leave the closet. We waited and waited. Late that evening, the rusty front gate creaked open. I breathed relief to see my mom standing there alive. Her black purse dangled as she held her arms open wide. Ed and I dashed into her embrace. Covering us with kisses, she said in a choked voice, "We're all fine. Thank you, God!"

A few days later, my father came home safely as well. Whoever was now in charge in the white presidential palace in downtown La Paz settled into power, supported by the nation's military. Life returned to relative calm as well. But we knew it was only a matter of time until the next revolution. In fact, the story of my family and how we'd ended up in our small stucco home up on a mountainside was birthed out of just one such revolution.

Chapter Two
Our Andes Home

Unless the LORD builds the house, its builders labor in vain.

—Psalm 127:1

The family of my maternal grandfather occupied a high position in Bolivian society, and in his younger years, my grandfather had been a respected diplomat for the ruling government party. When that regime was overthrown in one particularly violent revolution, my grandfather and other members of the defeated government were forced into exile in Peru.

That is where my grandfather met my grandmother. Abuelita was one of thirteen children born to a wealthy Peruvian family. Her light skin tone and hazel eyes testified to European blood, and like my grandfather's family in Bolivia, her family occupied a high position in Peruvian society. Their wealth came from a large amount of land they owned in a lushly tropical part of Peru.

Abuelita and her siblings each had their own nanny and reveled in a life that lacked nothing.

That all changed for Abuelita when she married my grandfather. Once Bolivia's unrest subsided, they traveled back to Bolivia, where my grandfather became an author, writing books about his experience as a diplomat. With bold audacity, the pages of his books detailed the corruption and flaws of Bolivia's political scene. As an author, Grandfather always had a passion to see things for himself. My mom can remember her father walking her down to the central plaza when she was only five or six years old. They followed the bloody trail in order to witness the ousted politicians who had been hung there as well as insurgents killed in the latest revolution.

But my grandfather's literary success didn't last long. Alcoholism took over, and his productive years came to an abrupt end. As his once-sharp mind declined under the effects of alcohol abuse, he became the black sheep of the family, losing all ability to make money, write, or work. Without provocation, he vented on anyone around, including his two sisters, whom he treated with harshness and insults.

Their vengeance came after the death of their parents when the family home was sold. The two sisters received most of the inheritance, leaving my grandfather only a small portion. Unfortunately, this wasn't enough to purchase a home down in the beautiful central valley where the more prosperous residents of La Paz lived. My grandparents had to purchase a stucco house in a lower-class neighborhood so high up the side of the surrounding basin it didn't even have a street address.

The house was originally built by a high-ranking government official with a large enough budget to hire plenty of household help. The family part of the house had three bedrooms, a sitting room, dining room, living room, library, tiny kitchen, and bathroom. The sitting room had a glass ceiling, a wonderful feature as bright sunbeams shone through the glass panes during cold Andes winters and warmed the room.

The house also had a garage and servant quarters. All the rooms were quite small compared to the wealthy homes in which both my grandparents had been raised, though the locals in that poor neighborhood considered it a mansion. Despite its small size and inconvenient distance from the city center, it had one feature with which Abuelita became enamored—its beautiful garden. Flowerbeds overflowed with red and pink geraniums, purple pansies, yellow and red roses. Manicured flowering bushes lined the paths. A fountain burbled joyously at the center of the garden's lower level.

Unfortunately, every centavo my grandparents possessed had been used to purchase the home. Like most poorer nations, Bolivia had no programs for social security, pension, or public assistance. And with my grandfather's alcoholism, my grandparents had no income except what they could get by renting out parts of the property.

The garage was rented to a couple who put up cloth curtains to divide their quasi-kitchen from their bedroom. The servant quarters were also rented to anyone able to pay rent. At one time, two women who tried to convince Abuelita to become a Mormon settled in those rooms. Since his alcoholism impaired my grandfather's judgment, Abuelita had to handle all their affairs, which was difficult considering she'd had no experience in finances, budgeting, or real estate before marrying my grandfather.

Their only child, my mom, grew up in that house. Highly intelligent, she finished high school and enrolled in the University of La Paz. When she was twenty years old, she met a young man in one of her classes. They fell in love and were married a year later. They moved into one of the bedrooms in my grandparents' home. I came along in 1952. Two years later, my younger brother Eduardo, or Ed as we came to call him, was born. As was common in poorer Latin American homes, all four of us shared the same bedroom.

Books were among the few treasures Abuelita brought to Bolivia when she married my grandfather, including classics by world-renowned authors like Jules Verne and Mark Twain. She stored these books in the library inside a bookcase with a glass door. On rainy afternoons, Abuelita often invited Ed and me to accompany her into the library.

"What do you want me to read today?" she would ask.

Ed and I usually chose Aesop's Fables. We waited with delighted anticipation as Abuelita opened the bookcase with a large key. She had covered a warped wooden chest with a thin, old cloth pad. Ed and I would sit beside her on this "sofa" while she read aloud to us.

Mom had inherited Abuelita's passion for reading, and she found work as a library assistant at the University of La Paz. Working on cars was Father's favorite hobby. But his forte was in numbers. He landed a job as an accounting clerk for a company that produced music records by local and national artists. Their combined salary was enough to purchase food and other necessities as well as pay the modest tuition for Ed and me to attend a private Catholic school.

While our parents worked, Abuelita prepared meals and provided childcare for Ed and me. Each morning after she fed the birds, she cared for her rose bushes. Sometimes she poured coffee grounds around them. If anyone in the family came down sick, she dashed out to cut leaves from her medicinal plants, which she steeped to make a tea that purported to cure everything.

A devout Catholic, Abuelita routinely gathered with other women during the week to pray the Rosary. On Sunday mornings, she always dressed in the black wool skirt she reserved for special occasions. When she grabbed her purse and small prayer book, Ed and I knew it was time to head to Mass.

"Where's your veil?" she would ask me.

I'd lift the white lacy covering for my head. "I have it here."

We held hands as we walked up the dirt hill to Gruta de Lourdes church. We always arrived well before Mass started. This gave us time to go to confession, a ritual I detested. I often invented sins as I assumed the priest would grow suspicious if the only sin I ever confessed was that I'd lied.

Once "cleansed" by receiving our assigned penance of reciting ten Hail Marys or four Our Fathers, we received Holy Communion.

The fact that Father's younger brother was a seminary student preparing to be a priest foolishly convinced us we were extra-special Catholics.

Although reading the Bible in those days was never encouraged, and even frowned upon by the Catholic Church,

Abuelita defied those rules and spent many afternoons on her bed with the cat beside her, reading her Bible. Later, her whistle alerted the family to gather for prayer. She always knelt on her bed facing the window while the rest of us knelt on the floor.

Abuelita prayed for everything. For funds to meet expenses. For God's help to endure my grandfather's violent temper. For protection from Bolivia's many political revolutions. Even for her two dogs, whom she named Kid and Toy, a testimony to her love for the English language.

Feeding the hungry was her ministry. No matter how little we had as a family, Abuelita always saved whatever vegetables she could to prepare a big pot of soup. On certain afternoons each week, a group of thin, malnourished people in tattered clothing gathered outside our worn-out, rusty gate, each holding a dingy, shapeless tin bowl.

While Kid and Toy barked furiously, Abuelita carried the pot through the gate. As the hungry crowd sat on the ground, patiently waiting their turn, Abuelita dipped a ladle into the pot and poured it into each bowl. The recipients didn't say much, but the look in their eyes expressed a pitiful but desperate, "Thank you."

CHAPTER THREE
BREAKING THE GLASS CEILING

Consider the ravens: they neither sow nor reap, they have neither storehouse nor barn, and yet God feeds them. Of how much more value are you than the birds.

—Luke 12:24

Although my parents worked hard, their salaries were modest, and house expenses continued to increase. The income from renting the garage and servant quarters barely covered the property taxes and utilities. Though the latter wasn't much since we only had electricity and water until noon each day.

With no money for upkeep, everything in our house stopped working one by one. The cracked walls with peeling paint stayed that way. When the toilet plumbing broke, we filled the bathtub with water and dipped this out with a bucket to flush the toilet. We couldn't complain at all since we were among the few houses in that area with the luxury of indoor plumbing.

The outside of the house also suffered. The previous owner had employed a full-time gardener to take care of the flowers, grass, and manicured bushes. We didn't have that luxury. The only parts Abuelita managed to care for were her rose bushes and the medicinal plants whose leaves she used for herbal remedies. Ornamental bushes turned to dry branches in the midst of weeds and debris. The water in the fountain became stagnant, a perfect playground for frogs.

So, there we were, all six of us in that once-beautiful home up a steep mountainside. With no funds for maintenance, both the inside and outside cried out increasingly for repairs as the decades slipped by. The Andes mountains looking down on our family home were silent witnesses of its slow decay, but our family dismissed this as just part of life.

Mom always looked at the bright side. If you asked her what she remembered about La Paz, she would probably say the beautiful snow-covered peaks. Or the deep blue of its cloudless sky. Or the brilliant glitter of stars that draws astronomers from all around the world. Because La Paz is set at such a high altitude and its atmosphere is so thin, the stars appear close enough to almost touch them.

But under that breathtaking canopy was the scenery I remember. The stucco walls, tiled roof, and many rooms of our house that were in stark contrast to tiny mud huts with thatched roofs. They scattered across the mountain slope amidst weeds, wildflowers, and rocks. Entire families with their sparse belongings lived packed inside those small quarters.

Through the years, more homes, a small Catholic church, a few apartment buildings, along with the military base, had filled up all available flat areas of the mountain slope around us. Around the corner from my house now stood a bright-pink apartment building where I often spent time playing with two friends who lived there.

Across the street from the apartment building was an undeveloped lot filled with weeds and rocks. An elderly woman in dingy, tattered clothes had claimed one corner where two mud walls met as her own. Little by little, she'd built a makeshift house there out of cardboard boxes and newspapers. Outside this flimsy home, she'd gathered her treasured belongings—bent, rusty pots and a collection of worn-out items she'd retrieved from the local dump. One glance at her as she moved slowly around her primitive quarters painted a picture of tangible despair, gloom, and the epitome of poverty.

On the flat portion of this same lot was the neighborhood playground. It featured monkey bars, swing, and slide. When going down the slide, we had to stay in the middle to avoid the sharp, rusted edges. The ropes holding the swing were worn out as if a mouse had climbed them and chewed off bites. The wooden swing seat was dried out and topped with splinters. They became a cruel reminder that sliding off was not a good idea. But Ed and I never gave a second thought to the condition of the playground. We just had fun.

For boys living in primitive hovels on the mountainside, a favorite sport involved making slingshots out of a forked branch and pieces of discarded rubber. Sometimes birds were their victims. Other times they climbed higher up the mountainside, which provided a clear view of our sitting room with the glass ceiling. This was an irresistible target, and the glass was eventually pockmarked with holes.

As our house continued to decay, the chaos inside increased as well. Years prior, one of Abuelita's sisters had died in Peru, leaving her daughter Laura an orphan. Without hesitation, Abuelita brought Laura to La Paz to live with them. She and Mom were both teenagers at the time, and it seemed an ideal solution since neither girl had any siblings for companionship.

But Laura's arrival soon showed its dark side. As a very young girl, Laura had witnessed her mother being forced into a cage and taken to an insane asylum. Her mother's death added to her trauma, leaving her emotionally and mentally unstable. With no counseling or meds, she became schizophrenic.

During our childhood there, Ed and I would hear Laura's screams for help from her room. She claimed someone was trying to poison her. At other times, she would go into fits of rage against my mom, insisting Mom wasn't my grandparents' biological daughter and wasn't part of the family. These accusations sparked Abuelita's desperate prayers for those lies to stop.

We ignored Laura's assertions because, after all, like my grandmother, Mom was light-complexioned with hazel eyes and European features. This fact emphasized Laura had to be deranged for suggesting Mom wasn't Abuelita's daughter.

Surprisingly, Laura displayed another personality outside the house around other people. She could be kind, sweet, and amazingly intelligent. One day she came home and announced that she'd found a job. Abuelita opened her eyes wide. "A job? Where? What will you be doing?"

Laura smiled widely. "I'll be a nurse at the hospital in Miraflores."

This was a government-run hospital that cared for the indigent. Looking up from the book he was reading, Grandfather raised his bushy eyebrows. "What do you know about nursing? You're going to kill those people."

He was right that Laura had no training or knowledge in the medical field. But conditions at the government-run hospital were terrible and finding medical personnel willing to work there was always difficult. So, the hospital was happy to give her a position even without any training.

Laura worked at first in the emergency room, then moved to other floors, treating and administering medication to patients. They all loved her kind, giving demeanor. But her career soon met a hiccup. One day she came home and announced she was pregnant.

Abuelita let out a scream and threw her hands in the air. "How could you?"

Grandfather spat out some colorful language and demanded that the man responsible come and face them.

"He can't do that," Laura protested. "He's a respected doctor at the hospital."

My grandparents insisted. A few days later, the doctor showed up. We all sat in our tiny living room while my grandparents shot questions at him like a firing squad. The doctor squirmed, whether because of the unfriendly looks the family darted at him or because he was sitting on the exposed springs protruding from our dilapidated couch.

Finally, the doctor said in a sheepish voice, "Well, after all, she's a nurse. I thought she was protected."

The only thing that could protect our family from the shame was to force a rushed wedding. We called the local priest, who without delay married Laura to the doctor. The house became even more crowded once the doctor moved in. But that didn't last long. Just a few weeks after the wedding, the doctor went off to work and never came back. I was ten years old when Laura's child was born and absolutely thrilled to help care for her. Laura continued to work at that hospital until she retired decades later with a government pension.

One reason I was so happy to pour out my affection on a cute baby was because I received so little from my own father. He was always stern, demanding and expected immediate and total obedience. I know now, looking back, that he was under great pressure trying to provide for the growing number of people living under our roof. Each revolution brought in a new government, possibly more corrupt than the previous. The change impacted everyone. One day a loaf of bread might cost one peso. The next day, it might cost ten pesos.

One afternoon, I looked frantically for the only pencil I owned. Homework needed to be done, and I had no pencil. When Father arrived from work, he frowned at me. "Did you do your homework?"

I swallowed the lump in my throat. "I...I lost my pencil."

He smacked my head. "How dumb is that? Go. Don't come back until you find it."

Tears flowing, I ran off to look for the pencil. I was too young to understand that my father was also looking for something—a way out of Bolivia. And just as urgently, to escape from the unrest in our own family.

Chapter Four
It'll Be Okay

And the same God who takes care of me will supply all your needs from His glorious riches, which have been given to us in Christ Jesus.

—Philippians 4:19

My younger brother was often the target of Grandfather's outbursts. I, on the other hand, received a smidgen of love from him. We both attended Catholic schools, his all boys and mine all girls. Without fail, Grandfather would wait for me at the corner where my school bus stopped. Mother Matilda was the nun in charge of the bus. Her job was to make sure each girl got out at the correct corner.

Sometimes Abuelita cut red roses from her bushes, wrapped the stems in newspaper, and handed them to Grandfather. "Here. These are for Mother Matilda."

Following Abuelita's instructions, Grandfather shuffled down several dirt streets to meet me. As the bus drew close to the corner, I peeked out the window. There he was wearing the wrinkled pinstripe suit he refused to remove even at night when he went to bed. The stains on his tie and shirt matched. His old, scuffed shoes had lost their shape, and he wore no socks.

"Perez, come to the front," Mother Matilda called out with the voice of a sergeant. "Your grandfather is waiting for you."

Once the bus door opened, Grandfather removed his worn-out hat, pressed it to his chest, and gave a slow but defined gentleman's bow as he handed the roses to Mother Matilda. Her black veil swayed as she extended her arm to receive them, giggling like a teenager. "For me?"

He smiled widely, showing the few teeth he had left. "Beauty only for the beautiful."

One of Grandfather's greatest skills was being able to recite at a moment's notice long poems by famous Spanish poets. Another ability he possessed was to make money—his own way. He began by selling the books he'd authored.

Once they were all sold, he moved on to other sale items. Anything at home that wasn't attached, he'd grab, slip inside his suit jacket, and leave the house. As he shuffled through the neighborhood, he always found someone to purchase those items.

This was a constant irritating thorn for my father as the few tools he'd gathered through the years disappeared one by one. The few kitchen utensils also vanished. Father, Abuelita, and my mom would protest, scold, and threaten him, hoping he would stop his antics.

But he never did. Instead, often with no provocation, he would shout profanities, slip off one of his old shoes, and hurl it through a windowpane. As glass shattered across the old wooden floor, my mom, brother, and I would escape into our bedroom for protection. The three of us sat on the bed, Mom hugging us tight. "It's going to be okay. He'll calm down soon."

Janet's parents in Bolivia.

He eventually did. But none of us could predict his next outburst, and we lived in dread of them. Hostility at home, fear of Grandfather's violent temper, low-paying jobs, and the unstable economy prompted my parents to consider leaving Bolivia. Everyone in Bolivia, including my family, expressed admiration for the wonders to be found in the United States. A country where dreams came true. Where prosperity and freedom could be found. These attractive attributes made the United States a logical choice to begin a new life.

But first we had to satisfy the stringent requirements imposed by the U.S. Immigration Department on anyone wishing to enter her borders and establish residency. One evening, my parents sat in our dark, tiny kitchen while Ed and I sat quietly at the table, scraping our plates clean of any remaining trace of rice.

"We have to do it," Father whispered to my mom. "We have to go to the United States."

Mom nodded, but her face held a troubled expression. "We'll have to pray, really pray, to find a way to raise the two thousand dollars they are asking for."

My parents' combined salary was only a hundred dollars a month, so this was almost two years of income. These funds deposited in a U.S. bank served a purpose. Should the family find themselves unemployed once they were in the United States, the money would be used for airline tickets to send them back to their native country.

In addition to the two thousand dollars, a long list of documents had to be presented to the American embassy. This included background details, references, and guarantee letters from reputable character witnesses in the United States as well as Bolivia.

None of these demands discouraged my parents. They stood hour after hour in line at the American embassy to turn in papers and receive more documents to fill out. My parents' salary barely covered school tuition, bills, and food, so we sold what furniture we could to pay the application fees.

"I have to get another job," Father announced one day. "A company is importing flour, and I can drive the truck to bring it in."

His day job in a recording company and night job transporting sacks of flour allowed Father to pay the immigration processing fees. Four years later right before my twelfth birthday, he walked into the house, waving papers in the air. With a huge grin, he kissed my mom. "We have them! They approved our visas!"

"Thank you, Lord!" Mom cried.

Some win the lottery. We had won something more valuable: entry into the United States. Our remaining challenge was to raise enough funds for airline tickets. Another expense seemingly impossible to meet.

But again, my father had a plan. As payment for mechanical work he'd provided, he had received a 1949 Willy's Overland military jeep. It didn't run, and the interior was falling apart. Every Saturday afternoon, Father slipped under it and worked on that old jeep. His mechanical work finished, he used a hand crank and started the engine. Then he found scraps of wood paneling to enclose the body of the jeep. This became our "luxury" vehicle. With no TV and little other entertainment at home, family drives into downtown La Paz were an absolute treat for Ed and me.

One Saturday afternoon, Father walked into the house, wiping his greasy hands with a rag. Sadly, he announced, "We're selling the jeep. We need the money."

But before he sold the jeep, Father put it to use for a different purpose. His plan was based on Bolivia's history. More than a century earlier in 1879, a war between Chile and Bolivia ended with Chile seizing Bolivia's only outlet to the sea. This moment in history when their nation was left landlocked would never be forgotten by the Bolivians. From early childhood, our teachers taught us the details of that awful injustice. This resentment fueled a victim mentality where economic, social, and political woes were frequently blamed on our lack of maritime access.

The desire to reclaim their outlet to the sea burned in the heart of the Bolivian people. My father devised a way to monetize that intense emotion. Finding one of many songs with lyrics clamoring the Bolivian dream of an outlet to the sea, he negotiated with the record company he worked for to produce records at minimal cost.

Next, he wired a speaker and affixed it to the roof of that old jeep. While the song played over and over again, he drove around the narrow cobblestone streets of downtown La Paz. Mom sat in the front passenger's seat with a pile of records on her lap. Ed and I sat in the back. A wide tear down the center of the worn-out vinyl seat made a perfect dividing line between us as we still fought constantly. Ignoring each other, we pressed our wind-cracked red cheeks against our respective windows, taking in the scenery.

The Jeep.

Outside the jeep, vendors and pedestrians jammed the sidewalks. Quechua and Aymara women wore indigenous attire—green, yellow, red, and brown skirts called *polleras* layered on top of each other until they stood out like a bell with white blouses under colorful shawls. Derby style hats covered the top of their black braids. They sat patiently behind piles of fruit and vegetables, hoping for a sale. Those with babies nursed them openly.

Ambulatory vendors carried large wooden trays supported by long straps around their necks. These overflowed with small items for sale—fingernail clippers, Bazooka gum, candy, peanuts, matches, batteries. As our jeep moved slowly down the street, some shoppers stopped their transactions to stare at us with curiosity. Others approached the jeep to inquire about the song. Rolling down the window, Mom would offer a record for purchase. Each time, the smell of exhaust from dilapidated buses mixed with a stench from the sewers wafted in. Ed and I didn't mind as we were too engrossed in the action outside.

Last family portrait taken in Bolivia.

My father's efforts paid off. Added to what we already had, the record sales brought in enough funds to satisfy the requirements of the United States Department of Immigration along with a single airline ticket. The plan was for my father to travel ahead of us to St. Louis, Missouri, and look for a job there, then send for Mom, Ed, and me once he'd earned enough money to provide for us and purchase additional airline tickets.

But his plans for departure met with swift opposition.

CHAPTER FIVE
DON'T TRY TO STOP ME

He guides the humble in what is right and teaches them his way.

—Psalm 25:9

On special occasions, we visited my father's oldest sister, Aunt Nelly, who lived with her husband, Uncle Jaime, in a new upper-class suburb of La Paz. Unlike our family, they had the financial prosperity to maintain their home and garden. Even their furniture was new, plushy, and comfortable, unlike ours. An interior courtyard was lined with beautiful flowers.

The house came alive when all the brothers and sisters gathered there with their spouses and children. My father and the other men would chatter in the patio while Mom and the other wives visited inside. Uncle Jaime's mustache danced on his lip with every bellow of laughter he let out. These increased with each cocktail he poured for himself and the rest of the uncles. In the background, Uncle

Jaime's shaggy dog Whiskey barked every time he heard a car engine passing down the street.

Sapo, or "frog," was my uncles' favorite game. A wooden table placed about six feet away was dotted with holes, each covered with a flapping metal door. The goal was to toss a heavy metal coin into a hole and score points. At the center of the table sat a metal frog with its mouth wide open. Getting the coin in the frog's mouth was the ultimate goal.

Each uncle held his cocktail in one hand and with the other took turns tossing that metal coin. The more they drank, the further their coin tosses were from the frog, often missing the table altogether. Could they be seeing double, compliments of the liquor?

On one visit soon after my father had completed his plans to travel to the United States, one of my father's brothers, Uncle Juan, patted Father on the back as they finished their game of *Sapo*. "Hey, you're not serious about going to the United States, are you?"

Father's frown showed his resentment over his brother questioning his judgment. Setting his drink on the table, he responded with a stern tone, "I am."

Uncle Juan shook his head. "What in the world will you do there? You don't even speak English."

My uncles took turns reminding my father of other men they knew who had tried to make a life in the United States but had failed and returned to Bolivia. Father said nothing at first, then gave them the same look he gave me when I disobeyed. "Stop that foolish talk. I've made up my mind. Besides, I'll never know whether I can make it if I don't try."

Aunt Nelly emerged into the courtyard with a tray of perfectly golden *salteñas*, a baked empanada filled with flavorful broth, spicy vegetables, and meat that was a favorite Bolivian delicacy. Setting down the tray, she turned to my father. "You have to think of your family. How will they adjust? None of you speak English, and your children will have no friends there or family."

With her chubby hands and perfectly manicured blood-red nails, she handed around plates and napkins. "Think about the mistake you're making."

Little did my aunt and uncles know that their comments, rather than dissuade my father, simply fueled his determination to provide a more promising way of life for our family. In May 1964, despite all the emphatic admonitions from family and friends about the risky, uncertain future he would face in a foreign country, Father left Bolivia for the United States. We soon received a letter that he'd arrived safely in St. Louis.

Back home, more opposition surfaced. One afternoon, the rest of our family had gathered at the table for tea. My grandfather sat in his usual chair next to a window he'd broken several months earlier. This opening had become a favorite entrance for a swarm of flies visiting from a nearby garbage dump. Grandfather was having one of his calmer moments. While the rest of us furiously shooed flies, he shakily dunked bread into his teacup, ignoring the insects as though they were his little black friends.

Abuelita sat across from Grandfather, spreading homemade orange marmalade on bread for Ed and me, who sat on either side of her. Mom sat at the other end of the table. As we were finishing our tea, she turned to Abuelita, her tone soft and tender. "We've made our final decision. We'll all be leaving soon to join my husband in the United States."

Abuelita halted her teacup midway to her lips, eyes wide with dismay. "What did you say? You don't mean permanently?"

Mom gave a long sigh and nodded. "We have to do it for the sake of our family's future. And now is the right time."

Abuelita dropped her cup onto the saucer with a clank. Tears spilled from her hazel eyes. "Don't leave me. You can't."

I wanted to plead with Mom that we couldn't leave my precious Abuelita with our mean grandfather. We just couldn't do that to her. But I kept those arguments to myself. Grandfather continued gumming his tea-soaked bread without saying a word. Either he didn't hear Mom's announcement, or he didn't care. Maybe both.

From that day on, Abuelita tried to reason with Mom to stay in Bolivia. I could read the anguish in both of their faces. Meanwhile, my father sent letters every few weeks detailing the wonders in the new country where he now lived. Without fail, each letter also gave instructions regarding the next step toward our preparations to join him. I suspect he also detailed the struggles he faced, beginning with his inability to speak English, the drastically different culture, and his intense loneliness. But Mom chose not to share these with me or my brother.

My parents had chosen St. Louis for their American dream because Mom had been captivated as a young girl by the books of famous Missouri author Mark Twain. The adventures of Tom Sawyer and Huckleberry Finn along the Mississippi River had sparked a dream in her to someday visit the locations she'd read about. What my parents didn't expect was how bitter St. Louis winters would be, which only added to Father's loneliness.

But as was his character, Father overcame each obstacle with determination and perseverance. A few days after arriving in St. Louis, he met another Bolivian who worked for a hotel unloading trucks. Since no English was required for this task, he rolled up his sleeves and began that job. He worked as many hours as they allowed him.

Within just seven short months, he managed to reach all the goals he'd set so we could join him. He rented an apartment, bought a bright green secondhand Volkswagen, and shopped for a few pieces of furniture from Goodwill. In his letters, he wrote about each new goal he'd achieved. Once he'd saved enough, he sent the funds to purchase airline tickets for Mom, Ed, and me.

We finally had all we needed to leave Bolivia. But would Abuelita let us go?

CHAPTER SIX
ADIÓS, BOLIVIA

Let the morning bring me word of your unfailing love, for I have put my trust in you. Show me the way I should go.

—Psalm 143:8

At last, the long-awaited day came for Mom, Ed, and me to board an airplane that would take us to reunite with my father. As we headed to the La Paz airport on December 11, 1964, I should have felt excited. Instead, sadness filled my heart.

I stuffed a copy of my favorite comic book in my carry-on bag, the only nonessential Mom allowed me to pack. Since our suitcases had to meet the weight limit, we had to constrain ourselves to clothing and other necessities along with a few treasured keepsakes.

Abuelita, her two dogs, my brother Ed, and I followed my mom as she dragged the suitcases out of the house. A dilapidated taxicab waited by the rusty gate. The driver tossed our suitcases in the trunk and slammed it shut. Abuelita hugged me with one arm and Ed with the other, her grip tight as though she planned to keep us with her. I didn't want to let her go either.

Mom wiped tears as she hugged her mother goodbye. "I'll make sure to write. We'll be okay, and so will you."

That didn't convince Abuelita. She gripped Mom's hands. "Please, please don't make this mistake. Don't go. Don't leave me."

We climbed into the cab. Even after the doors were closed and the driver started the engine, Abuelita hung onto the door handle. "I don't know what I'll do without you."

Ed began to cry. "I don't want to go."

Seeing Abuelita so sad made my chest hurt and my hands tremble. I wished I could comfort her as she'd comforted me when I was hurting. The further we got from the house, the louder Ed cried. "I don't want to leave my Abuelita!"

I could no longer hold back my tears either. I turned around to look back through the rear window. Abuelita was holding her embroidered handkerchief to her eyes. Then we turned a corner, and she was gone. I was already missing her sweet disposition and tender love. My memory drew out a familiar image of her kneeling with her Rosary in hand, praying for us.

With each new turn of the cab, typical scenes of our neighborhood came into view. Señora Sanjinez stood outside her house on the corner, broom in hand. The sun spotlighted a variety of colors in her dyed hair—red, dark-brown, light-brown as if she were still in the testing process trying to make up her mind. Except for a white wrinkled handkerchief peeking out of her sweater sleeve, she wore all black, even her shoes and thick stockings, as a sign of mourning for her husband, though he had passed away many years ago. She and other neighborhood women standing in front of their homes and visiting with each other were part of the familiar scenery.

So were the indigenous women in tattered clothing seated on street corners with a few meager sales items ranging from a few pieces of fruit or candy to loaves of unwrapped bread randomly arranged on top of old cardboard boxes. I knew all their names and even some details of their sad stories.

Seated between my brother and me in the back seat of the cab, Mom hugged Ed, trying to stop his crying. "You'll see, when we get to the United States, all will be beautiful."

But tears were spilling down her cheeks as well, and no matter how often she wiped her tears, more came. I wanted to console her, but I was hurting too. This wasn't a vacation. This was a forever leaving of everything that was familiar. Was our life in Bolivia that bad? Why did we have to leave? I couldn't understand why this had to be so painful.

As we turned another corner, leaving our neighborhood behind, I craned my neck, attempting to file every detail of the streets, buildings, and other familiar scenes in my memory. Maybe most people wouldn't consider all this very pretty, but it was all I knew. It was home, and I'd felt secure here. Even at twelve years old, I recognized this trip was permanent, and I had an unhappy premonition I might never see any of this again.

As we drove by the playground with its rusty slide and monkey-bars and threadbare swing, I noticed that the wind was moving the swing back and forth as if waving goodbye to me.

Everything else was still. Perhaps the neighborhood was also sad to see us go. I watched the swing until it disappeared from view, saying a silent good-bye, then placed that scene, too, in the files of my memory.

The cab drove us through the hilly, crowded La Paz streets and along hairpin curves zigzagging up the side of the mountain to the flat plateau above where the airport was located. We checked our suitcases and cleared security. As we boarded a small DC-4 for our first flight to Lima, where we would catch a larger plane to Miami, excitement began mixing with my sadness. I had never been on a plane before, and everything I saw around me was new and amazing.

But airplane travel in those days was not smooth, nor were cabins pressurized as they are now. The result was that a large percentage of passengers suffered nausea and vertigo. Maybe I was distracted enough taking in all the details of my first airplane flight, the interior of the plane, and the scenery far below us outside the porthole. But for my mom and brother, the trip wasn't kind to their stomachs, and they made frequent use of the paper bags provided for that purpose in the seat pockets in front of them.

Though I'd handled the airplane trip well, I was completely unprepared for what awaited us in Miami. None of us had slept much on the long flight. My body jerked as the airplane tires hit the runway with a hard thump, making my heart race. Then the plane's powerful brakes screamed, bringing the plane to a halt. We had made it safely.

Ed's face was still pale from the motion sickness, but he bravely pulled his own suitcase behind him. I dragged mine too, and we both followed Mom from the airplane into the Miami airport. I glanced around in awe. Unlike the small La Paz airport, this terminal was so enormous I felt like an ant. I'd never seen a building that clean either or with so many huge windows and such tall ceilings. Men in white shirts and black pants with badges directed the deplaning passengers as to where they should go next.

Making our way to the customs counter, we waited our turn in a long line. Behind the counter stood the customs agent. Compared to most Bolivian men, who were quite short, the agent loomed over us like a giant. His blonde hair and blue eyes looked to me like a painted statue instead of a real person. He wore a stern look as he searched each suitcase.

When our turn came, the agent unzipped Mom's suitcase, lifted out some items, then reached to the bottom and pulled out a plastic bag filled with *chuño*, the freeze-dried whole potatoes that were a traditional part of Andean cuisine. Soaked in water until soft, peeled, and cooked with sauteed onions and garlic, they were a favorite delicacy of my father's that wasn't available in St. Louis, so my mom had looked forward to bringing him this treat.

The agent lifted the bag in the air and turned it around slowly, his puzzled expression making clear he had no idea what these grayish-white lumps were. With his large fingers, he tried to squeeze the contents. Then he stopped, eyebrows knit together, and gave us a stern look. Rattling off a few words in English none of us understood, he tossed the bag into the large trash can beside him.

Mom's eyes opened wide in shocked dismay. "*No, señor, son para mi esposo* (No, sir, they're for my husband)."

As she said that, she retrieved the bag of *chuño* from the trash can and stuffed it back into her suitcase. The agent's voice grew louder as he grabbed it, threw it back in the trash, and proceeded to zip the suitcase shut. It was no use trying to argue. We had to say goodbye to the *chuño* Mom had so lovingly brought all this way for my father and hello to a commitment to learn the rules of this strange new country.

Chapter Seven
Strangely Wonderful

When my spirit grows faint within me, it is you who know my way.

—Psalm 142:3

P ulling our suitcases behind us, the three of us made our way through long corridors toward our next gate, where we would board our final flight to St. Louis. Mom did her best to read signs indicating the correct concourse for our gate. I was busy admiring the shiny tile and colorful carpets. There were even restaurants and shops displaying sparkling jewelry, clothing, purses, books, and other items behind huge glass windows. It all seemed more like a small city than an airport.

Suddenly, I faced something not so pretty. Mom had stopped at the top of a metal staircase. Unlike staircases in Bolivia, this one had grooved treads that were strangely alive, moving downward non-stop. On either side were black handrails that were also moving downward. People pushed past us, stepping onto the top tread, then riding the moving stairs down to the next floor below.

It was, of course, an escalator. But I'd never seen one before, and my frightened heart was asking, "We don't have to do that, do we?"

Ed had no such fears. Elbowing me out of the way, he announced, "I want to go first."

He stepped onto the top tread and was immediately swept downward. Mom took my hand and placed it on one of the moving handrails. "Here. Just take a step forward."

I quickly pulled my hand back. "No, I'm scared."

"We have to do this." Mom again took my hand and placed it on the handrail. "Just hold on tight and walk forward onto the first step."

My heart beat rapidly as I obediently walked forward, gripping the handrail tightly with one hand while dragging my suitcase with the other. I almost lost my balance, but I managed to get myself and my suitcase onto the steps. Once the escalator reached the lower level, I had another scare trying to get off before the moving steps could sweep me into the groove where they disappeared.

We continued down another corridor, where we encountered yet another out-of-this-world experience. We were still a few feet from a set of large glass doors when they magically, supernaturally slid open all by themselves. I was mesmerized as we walked through to the other side, wondering what kind of invisible people had opened them. The United States was truly another planet for me.

Reaching our gate, we boarded the plane to St. Louis. This was a much shorter flight. As we began to descend, Mom concentrated on fixing her makeup and putting on red lipstick since she would be seeing my father for the first time in seven months.

Arriving in St. Louis, we exited the airplane. Since this was long before 9/11, people were allowed to meet arriving passengers at the gate, and when we stepped from the jet bridge into the airport, we saw a large crowd gathered. Among them was my father waving at us with a huge grin on his face. We all hugged long and tight. Then we retrieved our luggage and headed outside through more magically moving doors.

December in St. Louis was far colder than in La Paz, and the chill bit through my sweater as Father led us to the parking lot. He stopped in the middle of long rows of parked cars. With another big smile, he looked down at Ed and me. "Okay, you have to guess. Which one of these do you think is our car?"

Ed and I glanced around. We immediately noticed a bright green Volkswagen bug. Ed was the first to remember that Father had mentioned purchasing that exact color of Volkswagen in one of his letters. He pointed to the bug. "It's that one, right?"And of course, it was. We examined the car in awe as Father loaded our luggage. It was shiny with no scratches or dents. The interior seats weren't ripped up or worn out like our jeep back in La Paz. Ed and I sat in the back seat, eyes glued to the windows as we admired our strange new surroundings.

Most bizarre were the streets, so completely unlike the noisy, congested streets of La Paz. For one, they were all paved and clean with no trash. The cars stayed inside marked lanes and followed each other in orderly lines. They stopped at red lights even when no traffic was coming the other way. But the strangest thing was the complete lack of pedestrians as though we were driving through a ghost town.

Green VW, the first car Janet's father bought in the United States.

"What happened to the people?" I asked.

Father chuckled. "It's wintertime. No one walks anywhere because it's too cold. Besides, everyone here has a car."

Everyone? I thought. *What a rich country!*

Ed's stomach was still protesting the airplane ride, and he occasionally stopped watching all the sights to clutch his stomach and moan.

"We'll be home soon," Father reassured him.

Mom kept turning her head from side to side, trying to take everything in. "It's all so beautiful. This is a blessed country."

Father agreed as he pointed ahead. "See those police vehicles on the side of the street? They're stopping cars to make sure they have their registration."

He slowed down as a uniformed officer signaled us to pull over. Pulling over, Father rolled down his window. The officer leaned down and spoke in English. Father handed the officer his driver's license. The officer walked away. Moments later, he came back and handed Father his license along with a piece of paper.

"Thank you!" Father said.

"Thank you!" Mom echoed.

It was one of the few English phrases they both knew. Mom glanced into the back seat toward my brother. "Ed's going to be sick. We need to hurry before he throws up in the car."

"I know. I'm going as fast as I can." Pressing down on the accelerator, Father passed several cars to our right. We finally arrived at the neighborhood where he had rented a third-floor apartment. Compared to our house in La Paz where the four of us had shared a single bedroom, this apartment seemed huge. Everything looked new and clean, and there were no broken windows. Even the few pieces of furniture looked new and luxurious though Father had purchased them secondhand from Goodwill.

A new car. A beautiful apartment. The United States was truly a dream come true.

Father introduced us to another Bolivian family who lived next door to us on the third floor. They'd already been in the United States for several years, and they became our teachers on the American way of life. Mom learned how to place coins in the washing machine in the laundromat and how to add soap. The stove and window air conditioner were both novelties as well.

But for Ed and me, the most amazing treat in our new home was the television set. You turned a knob, and a moving picture came on. It was like having a small movie theater of our own. Even though we understood nothing that was said, we sat there fascinated and hypnotized by this wonderful attraction.

A few days later, my parents sat at the kitchen table with our new neighbors, drinking coffee. Father related our ride from the airport, including the admirable police monitoring of vehicle registrations. The neighbor lifted his eyebrows. "Monitoring? Did the police officer stop you and give you a paper?"

"Yes, he did." Father got up and dug the paper out of a kitchen drawer.

The neighbor had learned enough English to be able to read the words written on the paper. He shook his head sympathetically. "The police weren't monitoring anything. What you have here is a speeding ticket."

Learning the hard way became the norm in our adjustment to this new culture. But I was completely unprepared for the next step I was about to face.

CHAPTER EIGHT
NO MORE COW'S TONGUE

For your Father knows what you need before you ask him.

—Matthew 6:8

My bedroom in that apartment felt cold, empty, and so very strange. In Bolivia, only the wealthiest people enjoy the luxury of having their own bedrooms. From the time I was born until coming to the United States at the age of twelve, I'd slept in the same room as my parents and brother. But in this new country where everything was as different from Bolivia as *chuño* from French fries, I had my own bedroom. So did Ed while my parents shared a third bedroom.

Yes, everything here was bigger, better, and more exciting. But I disliked this new sleeping arrangement that left me alone in my bedroom. There were many other strange differences to get used to. Ed and I learned all about putting ketchup on French fries. An odd combination but quite yummy. We also learned to eat hamburgers instead of cow's tongue. Once Ed and I started school, we had to adjust to eating lunch there instead of coming home for the midday meal.

Mom dove into her own adventure of grocery shopping. She was fascinated by the abundance packed onto the grocery store shelves. But even more fascinating was shopping indoors with beautifully displayed products one could touch and examine at leisure. No more open-air markets with cranky venders seated behind their piles of produce and scolding their customers if they touched the over-ripe tomatoes or fruit without purchasing them.

Like a kid in a candy store, Mom strolled through the grocery store aisles with their tall shelves filled with an endless variety of items. Because of her limited ability to read the English labels, shopping was a time-consuming process. Once she brought the groceries home, some items she pulled out of the paper bags were a mystery to the rest of us. Some of them delighted our taste buds such as Hostess apple pies. With no refrigerator available in La Paz, milk was always at room temperature, so getting used to drinking cold milk required effort.

But more effort had to be exerted to adjust to my new school. Catholicism had been the largest religious affiliation in St. Louis with Catholic churches and schools in virtually any neighborhood. Ed and I had attended Catholic schools in La Paz, and my father had already enrolled us in the parochial school that corresponded to our neighborhood, St. Roch Catholic School.

One morning shortly after our arrival, Ed and I were delighting in another novelty of American life, a bowl of scrumptious Captain Crunch cereal. While we crunched our way through the last bites and practically licked the bowl, Father made an announcement.

"Listen, both of you. We all need to learn English as soon as possible. The fastest way for you to learn is by going to school. I've registered you both, and you'll be starting on Monday."

"Monday?" I echoed in dismay. "So soon?"

Father frowned at me sternly. "Don't argue with me. The sooner you start learning English the better."

Janet and her brother, Ed, ready for the first day
at Catholic school in the United States.

Ed and I both knew better than to talk back to our father, so we made no further protest. That Monday morning, all four of us bundled up against the cold December morning and climbed into the Volkswagen bug. St. Roch Catholic School was only a few minutes' drive from our apartment. As we walked through the front doors, Father turned to Ed and me. "You do whatever they tell you, do you hear me?"

We nodded. Disobeying our father in any way was something else Ed and I would never dream of doing. My parents walked the two of us into the office of the school principal, a nun named Sister Katherine. The black habit and veil she wore contrasted sharply with her pale face, very different from the brown complexions of the Bolivian nuns I'd known. Her nose was long and pointed. I thought irreverently that maybe Pinocchio was her close relative.

In St. Louis, a midwestern city, Latin American immigrants or even native Hispanics were rare. And in 1964 there were no ESL (English as a Second Language) programs to help us or interpreters to come to our rescue. Since Sister Katherine spoke no Spanish, my father had to make the introductions with his limited English. Once my parents left, Sister Katherine curled a long, bony finger at Ed and me and began to speak. When she got no answers from us, she must have finally realized we didn't speak English.

Beckoning us to follow, Sister Katherine led us in complete silence through the school hallways. She eventually stopped outside a classroom door. She knocked, then opened the door and motioned me to enter. The teacher, a shorter version of Sister Katherine, pointed to an empty desk in the back.

I had attended Catholic schools in Bolivia, so the nuns were familiar to me. What was painfully unfamiliar were the dozens of eyes staring at me as I walked between the rows of desks to take my seat. Unhappy reality gripped me as I realized how different I must look to my new classmates. All the other sixth-graders were dressed alike in their school uniforms, while I wore the skirt and sweater I brought with me from Bolivia. Their desks had books, pencils, and notebooks. I had nothing on mine.

What a relief when the nun clapped her hands and said something that caused the other students to turn their eyes to the front. But when recess came, a group of girls circled around my desk. Pointing at me, they whispered and giggled. The tallest girl in the circle had blonde curls that bounced when she giggled. I bit the inside of my lip to help me hold back tears, doing my best to ignore their ridicule.

Months later, I learned that my pierced ears and tiny gold earrings were what had evoked such a reaction. In Latin America, piercing a baby girl's ears was as common as giving them herbal tea in their bottle. But in 1964, girls with pierced ears were still an oddity in the United States.

When I got back to our apartment, Mom wrapped her arms around me and asked tenderly, "How was your first day?"

That did it! Releasing my pent-up tears, I burst into a torrent of sobbing. When I finally caught my breath, I begged, "Don't make me go back!"

Her tight hug and tender words of reassurance were all I needed to comfort me. I lingered in her embrace for a bit, then wiped my tears. "Don't tell Father. He'll get mad at me."

The next day, Ed and I walked to school on our own, using houses and yards we'd passed the day before as landmarks. I felt more comfortable once I received a school uniform and my textbooks. But that comfort didn't last long. A few days later, I brought a note home. Mom, always diligent in following instructions, read the note with the help of a dictionary. "It says we need to buy you short pants to wear in gym class."

In Bolivia, no one wore short pants. After consulting our Bolivian neighbors for necessary details, Mom and I headed to Sears to shop for my new short pants. Spotting shorts among the clothing racks, we purchased a pair. The next day, I put them on under my uniform skirt.

When the time came for gym class, all the girls removed their skirts. When I slipped mine off, the other girls stared at me. Then a roar of laughter echoed all across that large gym. Instead of navy blue gym shorts like all the other girls wore, I was wearing blue and green striped bloomers.

Pulling my skirt back on, I ran to the bathroom. I wanted to hide there forever, but the gym teacher came after me and took me to the office. Her smile told me that she sympathized with my humiliation. When I sat down, she patted my hand kindly. We soon learned that the proper gym shorts had to be purchased at the same school store as our uniforms.

Ed's reactions to his new school were very different from mine. He didn't care about fitting in as long as he could play ball. Even at eleven years old, he was skilled in sports, and he quickly won friends by scoring goals on the soccer field. But like me, Mom also struggled to make her way in this new culture. Though Father had a good job unloading trucks for a large hotel, Mom felt impelled to find work as well, and she didn't consider lack of fluency in English as an excuse for being unemployed.

A yellow Spanish-English dictionary became Mom's best friend. Referring to it often, she translated a want ad for a library assistant at St. Louis Community College. She took a bus to the college office, where she would need to take a typing test to apply for the job. In Bolivia, Mom always won the hearts of everyone she encountered, whether at work, social settings, or in the neighborhood. She was also greatly admired for her work ethic, including her typing skills.

The problem was that in Bolivia she'd always used a manual typewriter. In America, manual typewriters were practically extinct. For the test, she was assigned an electric typewriter. She pressed a key. To her astonishment, the letter printed all the way across the page.

But Mom didn't give up. If she could dodge bullets in Bolivia's revolutions, she could use this typewriter. And she did. But the interview that followed tested her further. She smiled each time she didn't understand what the interviewer was asking. She finally took a deep breath and told the interviewer firmly, "I work, you like, you pay. You no like, you no pay."

The interviewer paused, grinned, and gave her the job on the spot. As the years swept by, Mom became completely fluent in English. Her vivacious personality and work ethic garnered the admiration of her colleagues and superiors until she retired twenty-five years later.

"God is so good to give me this job," Mom would tell her friends. "But the best blessing is that college tuition is free here for my Janet and Ed."

Father also moved on to better positions. Like Mom, he sought out work with English-speaking colleagues to sharpen his English.

Eventually, the St. Louis winter turned into the green grass and flowers of spring. Flowers of hope were blossoming in me as well. A few girls walked home on the same path I did. I tried out some words in English with them, then some phrases. As time went on, these became full sentences. I was also understanding more and more English.

Kathy, a girl with curly brown hair and huge green eyes, became my closest friend. From the beginning, she used hand gestures to invite me to sit beside her at lunch. At first, I said nothing while I pulled out my liverwurst sandwich on Wonder Bread. But she just smiled at me, no words needed. Her kindness warmed my heart and gave me the encouragement I so sorely needed. To this day, Kathy and I remain close friends.

Father began a new routine at dinner time. He would test Ed and me to see how much English we had learned. To make sure we used the new words, he insisted the family speak English at home. This was awkward for me at first as I didn't have enough vocabulary to express myself. But none of us dared go against Father's decrees. And the sacrifice paid off. As months went by, my family was soon more fluent in English than our Bolivian neighbors who had been in the United States for years.

We quickly developed a routine for everything. Even for church attendance. Every Sunday Mom affixed a white lacey "veil" on the top of my head with a bobby pin, and we all headed to Mass. Obeying the doctrines of our Catholic faith was a priority. That Father's youngest brother in Bolivia had been ordained as a priest made us extra proud Catholics.

But sometimes during Mass, I saw tears dribbling down Mom's cheeks. Could she be hiding heartache? Did she miss Abuelita? Was her job too demanding? I never knew and never asked. But what I was about to find out would certainly be reason enough for Mom to shed more tears.

Janet's uncle, an ordained priest.

Chapter Nine
Starless Nights

All my longings lie open before you, O LORD; my sighing is not hidden from you.

—Psalm 38:9

One evening, I heard my parents whispering as they were seated at the kitchen table. When I walked in, they stopped. Father turned to me and asked, "Did you understand what the doctor said?"

I nodded, reviewing in my mind's eye the ophthalmologist visit I'd had earlier that day. It was the first vision test I've ever had since I'd never needed glasses. Sitting in the adjustable chair, I'd placed my chin on a metal rest while the ophthalmologist shone a bright light in my eyes.

"Try not to blink," he ordered.

After examining each eye, the ophthalmologist was silent for a moment, then turned to my parents. "She has inherited the retinitis pigmentosa gene. The effects could be serious. Many people with this gene lose their sight completely. Others don't. There's no way to know for sure at this point. And unfortunately, there is no cure or treatment."

Retinitis Pigmentosa? What a strange name, as unfamiliar to me as the vision test itself. The ophthalmologist explained that retinitis pigmentosa, or RP, is a disease of the retina where the rods and cones, which are responsible for detecting light and color, slowly deteriorate. In some cases, they halt their function completely. When this happens, blindness occurs.

My father had inherited this gene. Though he wasn't yet forty years old, he'd noticed that his night vision was diminishing. The ophthalmologist had confirmed that this was due to the RP gene deficiency and was the beginning of night blindness. Ed's eyes showed no sign that he had the gene, but I'd inherited it from my father. I was relieved when the ophthalmologist explained that I very likely wouldn't see any effects until perhaps the age of sixty.

"But I didn't understand what the doctor meant by night blindness," I said. "What is that?"

Mom turned toward me. "It means you can't see as well as other people when it's dark, even when there are lights. That is why your father is having difficulty driving at night because of his poor night vision. And even lights can be hard to see if they aren't quite bright. For example, seeing the stars at night isn't easy for those with poor night vision or night blindness."

Stars? I was puzzled. I knew what stars were from studying astronomy and seeing pictures. But I suddenly realized I'd never

ever actually seen any stars in a night sky. And I did bump into objects more often once dusk fell. But I'd always blamed those incidents on my clumsiness.

No wonder my parents were whispering about this, knowing that this dire prognosis could be a possibility for me and my father as well. Walking over to stand beside my mom, I said earnestly, "I can see just fine."

A tear fell from her hazel eyes as she lifted my hand and kissed it. "I don't want you to worry, honey."

And I didn't. After all, the ophthalmologist had said I probably wouldn't have any trouble with my eyes before the age of sixty. And to a thirteen-year-old, sixty seemed a lifetime away. My immediate future held countless opportunities to enjoy the company of my new friends, listen to music with them, go for walks to the local shopping plaza, or go to teen dances, an activity I found especially exciting.

By this point, we'd moved to a better neighborhood. The prior one had become quite rough. One day Ed came home crying with a bloody nose. Some older kids had tried to steal his lunch money, and Ed had learned the hard way that fighting back was not a good idea. St. Roch Catholic School only went through eighth grade so Ed and I would eventually have to transition to a new school anyway.

My parents rented a modest apartment near St. Mary Magdalen Church, which also had a parochial school. The rent was low enough to allow my parents to continue putting part of their income into savings. Their commitment to meet the financial goals they'd set before leaving Bolivia never wavered. They put nothing on credit and never missed a bill payment. They always managed to budget for tuition at the Catholic school for Ed and me as well as to put money aside for our college education. The one luxury they saved for was our annual one-week vacation at the Lake of the Ozarks.

My English continued to improve. This made life easier, and opportunities to learn something new came often. I'd become close friends with a girl named Maggie since we always walked back and forth to school together. One afternoon when we reached Maggie's front door, she told me, "My mom is making a cake. Wanna come in?"

Her mom smiled warmly at us as Maggie and I stepped into the kitchen, and her eyes held a kindly twinkle. I was astounded to see that one eye was blue and the other green. A person with two different colors of eyes was a first for me.

Maggie and I stood beside the kitchen counter, watching the cake making process. Her mom opened a box, emptied it into a bowl, added an egg and some oil, then whisked the mixture until smooth. To my shock, that was it. Pouring the mixture into a pan, she slipped it in the oven. That cake was the best I'd ever tasted. Back in Bolivia, Abuelita had made cakes on special occasions like birthdays. But this involved a long list of ingredients, then much work in preparing the mixture before putting it in the oven. Not so in the United States. Even cake preparation was easier and faster here.

But my diminishing night vision was most certainly not a piece of cake. The dimly lit gymnasium where my friends and I attended teen dances introduced me to the severity of my night blindness. I still remember the awful humiliation of one dance in particular. When the first notes of "My Girl" played, we girls all eagerly hoped a boy would ask us to dance. To my delight, I was one of the lucky girls who felt a tap on the shoulder. When I turned around, a boy extended his hand, inviting me to dance.

The slow dances were fine. But when we were dancing to a fast song, my dance partner and I moved to the rhythm individually. The lighting was so low that I lost sight of my partner and inadvertently ended up with my back to him. I didn't realize what had happened until other kids all around me began to laugh. Suddenly, I felt a pull on my arm. It was Maggie.

"You were dancing all by yourself," she told me. "He walked away when you weren't facing him."

My cheeks burned, and I fought to hold back tears. I shrugged it off at the time, but that night in my bedroom, I let the tears flow, vowing to never go to another dance. That vow didn't last as my passion for dancing soon put a band-aid on my humiliation. But from then on, I only accepted invitations to slow dance.

When navigating at night, I also came up with a plan. Each time my friends and I crossed a street at dusk, I held on to one of them. They didn't mind as they felt badly when I tripped or ran into an object. By the time I was in high school, I'd come to accept my lack of night vision.

What was more difficult to accept were comments from some of the boys in my class. I remember one in particular. I was standing in front of my locker when a boy paused as he was walking by to whisper in my ear. "Hey, Bolivian bombshell!"

I was horrified at his words. Any mention of bombs or gunfire took me back to Bolivia's frightening revolutions. And he'd used a word that had that connotation. Decades went by before I learned that "bombshell" was slang for an attractive young woman. The boy had actually been paying me a compliment.

My high school years were filled with intense, diligent study. My efforts paid off because my name was consistently on the honor roll. Admittedly, my interest in boys was equally consistent. My first boyfriend, Steve, walked into my life my junior year. We were too young to understand true love, but he was comfortable with my night blindness, and for that I was grateful.

Janet's last birthday as a Bolivian.

Another far more important event occurred that same year. By then, my family had fulfilled the five-year commitment of residency in the United States, and we were ready to apply for citizenship. We studied for the test, which we all passed with flying colors. My parents filled out the required documents. Eventually, we received the date for our citizenship ceremony. Dressed in our Sunday best, the four of us stepped into the hush of the courtroom. A red, white, and blue flag covered the front wall. With joy, honor, and gratitude, we raised our right hands to renounce our citizenship to Bolivia and declare our allegiance to the United States of America.

On the way home, Mom cried out, "I can't believe God is so good to us. We're now American citizens."

When our naturalization papers were drafted, we had the option to change our names. And we did. Eduardo became Edward, though we've always called him Ed. My name was changed from Jeanette to Janet. I liked the simpler spelling of my new name.

"We're Americans now," Father told us firmly. "So, I never want to hear any of you speaking Spanish in the presence of those who don't understand it. The language here is English. Only English."

As with all his decrees, Father made sure we obeyed that rule. He and Mom set examples for Ed and me of hard work, ethical behavior, honesty, and diligence in following the Catholic faith. Those prayers during Mass came in handy when I ended up in the hospital my junior year.

This was because I'd overindulged in a new delicacy. A friend had invited me to her house to spend the night, where she introduced me to a number of delicious snacks I'd never tasted in

Bolivia. Among these was cheese spread on Ritz crackers. My taste buds exploded in celebration. I must have devoured an entire box. Ham sandwiches were another treat I'd never enjoyed in Bolivia. We reveled in these and other treats without reservation.

Sadly, my digestive system protested at the drastic change of diet, resulting in an emergency appendectomy. Once recovered, I went on to my senior year of high school and then to college. Little did I know a degree wasn't the only reward awaiting me at that university.

CHAPTER TEN
RELEASING THE SECRET

O LORD, you have searched me and you know me. You know when
I sit and when I rise; you perceive my thoughts from afar.

—Psalm 139:1-2

After high school, I completed a two-year associate degree at
the community college where Mom's job provided me with
free tuition. During this same time period, another very special
change came into our home. My grandfather had passed away just
three years after we'd left Bolivia. We'd spoken on the phone with
Abuelita and other family members, but finances had never
permitted a trip back to Bolivia.

Now my parents made arrangements for Abuelita to relocate
from La Paz to the United States. After all the tears shed when we'd
said goodbye, what a special day it was when Abuelita was reunited
with her only daughter and her arms were once again embracing

her grandchildren. She would end up living with us in the United States until she passed away at almost a hundred years old.

And now I too was headed to new and bigger horizons—a four-year university—thanks to my parents' sacrificial saving so Ed and I could have a college education. One hot August day, my closest friend Trish and I began packing all the items needed to begin our college life. As was typical for the early 1970s, we both wore long hair to our waists and were dressed in hot pants and halter tops. I was a bit jealous that Trish's hair was naturally straight. Getting rid of the waves in mine required much time and effort.

But more than our appearance, we were preparing our hearts for the exciting adventure of being coeds at Southeast Missouri State University, about two hours from St. Louis. Trish looked at our pile and announced, "Yup, we can fit it all in my mom's van."

I tossed a bag of cassettes on top of the pile. "I hope I didn't forget anything."

In the end, I'd remembered to pack everything I needed. What I did try to forget were my feelings of inadequacy, the same ones I'd held when I first moved to the United States. My high school years had helped me mature, accept who I was, and learn to have fun with friends. Much like I fit into my bell-bottom pants, I now felt quite comfortable in my new American way of life.

What didn't feel quite right was the silly homesickness that began even before Trish and I hit the road. But would I voice those immature feelings to anyone? No way! I tried to convince myself all would be okay. But in moments when I was alone, the worrying began. If only I didn't have to worry about this nagging night blindness, I told myself, then I'd be like my friends overflowing with anticipation for university life.

I tucked my renewed feelings of inadequacy inside and did my best to forget them as Trish and I headed down the highway, the van overflowing with our stuff. The stereo blared a John Denver song as we pulled in our dorm's parking lot. We spotted some male students tossing a football outside a frat house. The landscape was looking good. Their toned muscles and flirty looks made Trish and me both smile.

Of course, I considered that my heart still belonged to Steve, who had stayed behind in St. Louis to work as an electrician. Neither of us had made a firm commitment to remain in a relationship during the two years I'd be away at college. But we were both confident we'd end up together someday.

For the moment, I decided to focus on my new season at college. My daytime vision was still clear with no impairment. So, I decided that exploring the campus was my first priority. I just needed to finish my exploration before dusk set in. Should night catch me outside, I'd be lost and would never make it back to the dorm without assistance. What an awful start that would be to my school year. I was determined to make sure such a humiliation never happened.

Trish and I unloaded the van, which turned our dorm room into a crowded maze of piled-up boxes and clothing. By the time we'd unpacked, an afternoon sun filtered through the yellow and green flowered curtains covering the small dorm window.

Looping my long, black hair into a scrunchie, I slipped into my flip-flops and headed out with Trish and some other new friends to explore the college campus. It was several hours later before we headed to the cafeteria for dinner. I breathed a sigh of relief that we'd arrived back before dusk.

After dinner, Trish and I returned to setting up our dorm room. By now the blackness of night was peering in the window, and lights blinked on all around the campus. As we arranged our belongings, Trish suddenly asked, "Hey, a bunch of us girls are going over to hear that group that's performing tonight. Are you coming with us?"

"No, I'm kind of tired," I responded. "I think I'll just stay here. Besides, I'm not into that kind of music."

What a lie! The group's singing thrilled me. And I would have absolutely loved to be out with my friends and potentially meet new ones. But I couldn't risk running into someone, falling down steps, or stumbling into objects. The streetlights provided enough lighting for everyone else but not for me. After repeated insistence that I join them, Trish and the other girls finally gave up and left. Sitting down on my new lavender bedspread, I hugged the pillow, hating my bad luck. Why did this disease have to happen to me? My brother hadn't inherited it, so why me? Tears rolled down my cheeks, and self-pity surged up inside me.

"Honey, not being able to see at night isn't the end of the world," Mom had told me when she began noticing my constant "accidents" where I ran into people, furniture, and even walls because the lighting was too dim for me. "Besides, just remember what the doctor said. You'll be fine for many years still."

But I wasn't fine. I was miserable, lonely, and angry. After a couple of weeks, I was forced to make a decision. A guy in my humanities class asked me out. My palms grew sweaty. Should I let him know about my night blindness? I ended up turning him down with a smile and gentle words. But he just asked me again the next day. When I said no again, he kept persisting.

Finally, I blurted out the truth. "I have night blindness, so it's better for me not to go out on dates."

I thought telling him the truth might dissuade him once and for all. But to my shock, he shrugged his shoulders. "No big deal. If you have trouble seeing, just hold on to me."

Hold on to him? I wasn't fond of him enough for that. But the possibility was inviting. If I declined, my dating would be limited to daylight only.

Everything changed a few weeks later. I was walking down the hall toward the cafeteria when I spotted a male student in a wheelchair. Unable to use his hands, he pushed his wheelchair backwards with one foot to transport himself from class to class. As he turned a corner, his books slipped out of his bag. I rushed to pick them up. Tucking them back into the bag, I patted his thin, gnarled hand. "No problem. The books are back where they should be."

A hint of a smile curved his mouth despite sharp, jerky movements of his head. That smile planted reality in me. This young man didn't seem to mind his appearance or the awkward way he had to maneuver around campus. Nor did he hide in his room.

I took that image back with me to my own dorm room, where my perceived disability glared at me as I looked into the mirror. I'd allowed my insecurities to build walls that blocked out opportunities and instead locked me inside with my own grief and self-pity.

The following week, the guy in my humanities class asked me out again. This time, I accepted. With that date, a whirlwind of dating began. Each guy provided just enough assistance to navigate me through places with dim lighting. While I never ventured out alone, dating gave me the freedom to go out at night.

But the real freedom was releasing the secret I had stored in my heart. I learned then that a secret not shared is a pain not healed. Still, even though I'd grown more comfortable with my college life, every phone conversation with Mom reminded me I was far from my family. I especially missed my mom. When I heard her voice, a lump would form in my throat, making it hard to hide my homesickness.

Of course, Mom knew me well enough to hear in my voice what I wasn't saying. She always finished our phone calls by reminding me, "Remember to go to bed early and get enough sleep."

She never bothered reminding me to study because she knew how determined I was to get good grades. Instead, she had a different admonition. "Remember, even if other girls don't have high standards, you do. You set the boundaries always."

I understood. Though the attention from college guys helped make up a little for my father's lack of affection, I always remained true to Mom's advice. I remembered her words when dorm life became challenging. Since cell phones didn't exist then, there was just one phone in the hall for all twenty girls on our floor to share. One girl named Betty seemed especially determined to be unfriendly. It didn't help that I was popular enough with male students to receive far more phone calls asking for dates than she did.

If she picked up the phone and the caller asked for me, she would shuffle down the hall to my room and knock sharply on the door. When I opened the door, she would say sneeringly around the Winston cigarette that always hung from her lips, "Perez, the phone is for you again."

Addressing another girl by her last name was as rude in American culture as in Bolivian culture. But she always did so, and her resentment was as evident as the smoke from her cigarette.

During these college years, being different from the other girls still seemed to be my pattern of life. An occasional kiss good night was the absolute limit of what I permitted from my dates. Meanwhile, my friends all told stories about their experiences with their boyfriends. The fun nights they spent together. The adventures of going camping together. The "beer busts" they attended.

In contrast, my friends informed me I was a total bore since none of these activities attracted me. My sole priority was to get straight A's. My one leisure time passion was going dancing with friends. Little did I know that even my tame dating experience would soon come to an abrupt halt.

CHAPTER ELEVEN
THE MAN GOD CHOSE FOR ME

The LORD directs the steps of the godly. He delights in every detail of their lives.

—Psalm 37:23

Steve, my boyfriend since my junior year in high school, and I had agreed to date other people while I went away to college. During that time, our love for each other continued to simmer. After five years of romance, we were certain we were meant for each other. The only thing left was to take the next step.

On Christmas Eve during my last year of university, Steve gave me a small box wrapped in gold paper. "Merry Christmas. Will you be my wife?"

My heart raced as I removed the gold paper. Inside was a marquise diamond ring. I didn't hesitate in my response. "Yes!"

Starting that night, my dating days were over. Just a week later on a cold St. Louis New Year's Eve, my friend's basement echoed with laughter and chatter as our college group celebrated the end of another year. But the night was even more special for me and Steve since this was also our engagement party. A colorful cake sat in the middle of the table. On it in red letters was written, "Congratulations, Janet and Steve!"

My friend Trish lifted my left hand. "Let me see that rock again."

Sadly, our engagement lasted only one week. In the middle of the party, Steve and I got into a fight. Without hesitation, I took my engagement ring off and gave it back to him. I shouldn't have been so hasty. Steve immediately left the party, and I was left with embarrassment and guilt. I packed those emotions in the suitcase of my heart and went back to college for my final semester.

I must have cared for Steve more than I realized because losing him devastated me. When I got back to my dorm room, I gathered up all the gifts, cards, letters, and everything else Steve had given me and threw them all away. I was done. I vowed to do what any immature coed does when a guy breaks her heart. I decided to look into becoming a nun.

My plan for pursuing my new goal was to check out the local Catholic church. But my immature, shallow whim didn't last long. As gossip goes, the news about my disastrous break-up with Steve during our engagement party spread like wildfire through my college dorm. Two days later, a friend in that dorm stepped into my room. "Janet, I heard what happened."

I tried not to blush. "It was probably for the best. But I'm done dating now. I want nothing more to do with guys as long as I live."

"I don't believe that," she said. "Anyway, there's someone who's been wanting to meet you. His name is Gene. He's my boyfriend's roommate, and he's perfect for you. Now that you're not with Steve, you should meet him."

I rolled my eyes. "Not interested."

She insisted. I listened as she described how handsome he was. Before long, I was seriously considering the possibility. Quicker than you can say disco, my plan to become a nun went out the window. Two days later, she introduced me to Gene. He invited me out.

"I need to tell you something," I said as we stepped out of my dorm building, trying not to stare too hard at his beautiful blue eyes. "I have night blindness so I may have to hold on to you when we're in dark places."

He gave a light chuckle. "No problem."

Gene never asked any questions. During our first date at a local disco club, he proved to be a gentleman, as eloquent and courteous as he was attentive to leading me in dimly lit places. The next week, he took me to a fifties party hosted by his fraternity. We chatted as we danced, and I learned he was born just twelve hours before me. His mom and mine were in labor at the same time, his in the United States and mine in Bolivia. We both turned twenty-two that year.

After we celebrated with a nice dinner, he turned serious. "I just want you to know something. You need to make a choice. Either you and I are seeing each other exclusively or not at all."

I chose Gene. We saw each other every day. Since my main focus was to get straight A's, I spent a lot of time in the library studying. If he wanted to see me, I made clear he'd have to spend time there too. And he did. The result was improved grades, and he ended up graduating with honors.

During the first months of our relationship, we learned the differences and similarities about each other's upbringing. Both of us were born into the Catholic faith. My family was close to each other and devoted to Catholic doctrine. His parents divorced when he was a young boy, and the family didn't actually practice any religion.

I'd also stayed with my parents until I left for college. In contrast, Gene became independent right after graduating high school. He'd learned to manage his own finances while I knew little about managing money or budgeting. Subconsciously, I'd embraced my parents' mindset that money should be spent only on necessary items. In contrast, Gene had witnessed his father and new wife enjoying recreational items like motor homes and boats.

During our first three months of dating, I thought we had learned all there was to know about each other. The next step was to bring Gene to meet my parents in St. Louis. After dinner, while we were sitting in the family room, he did something I wasn't expecting. Turning to my parents, he said with solemnity, "I want you to know that I love your daughter and would like your permission to marry her."

Permission to marry me? I was as surprised as my parents. My surprise turned to shock when Gene pulled out a red velvet box with a diamond ring inside. My parents were speechless. Only three months prior, I'd been engaged to someone else. Once again, my answer was a delighted *yes*.

But the final surprise didn't come from Gene. It came from my parents. Entering my bedroom one day before I returned to college, Mom gave me her bright, warm smile. "Janet, we could give you a graduation party. But that would last only a short time, and you'd soon forget it. So your father and I would like to send you to Europe as your graduation present."

I stared at her. I was in love and looking forward to organizing the details of my wedding as soon as Gene and I graduated from university. The thought of traveling didn't fit into my plans. "Europe? You don't have to do that. You paid for all my college. That's more than enough. Besides, I don't want to travel by myself."

Mom sat beside me on the bed. "You may never again have this opportunity to visit other countries. Maybe a friend can go with you."

I called Gene, who had already returned to campus. "You won't believe this, but my parents want to send me to Europe as a graduation present."

"That's fantastic!" He paused. "Just don't fall for any of those French guys and decide to stay over there."

We both laughed. In the end, Mom was right. A friend who'd graduated a year prior had saved her money and was eager to join me. And that Europe tour was an adventure that still makes me smile with delight when I remember those memories.

Once I came back, Gene and I got busy planning the details for a wedding in January of the following year. Like any passionate Latina, I focused on planning the wedding, music, and reception. But I hadn't really thought much about the marriage itself.

The big day came. Six bridesmaids in burgundy velvet dresses lined up in the back of St. Mary Magdalen Catholic Church. My wedding dress was perfect for a winter wedding. I wore a white cape that contrasted with my long black hair. At the reception, everyone danced to Bolivian music and American tunes. Leaving the celebration, Gene and I headed off to our honeymoon.

But shortly after the honeymoon, all celebration stopped. Once we entered into a routine, the contrast in our upbringings became painfully obvious. We'd fallen into the misconception that our love would be enough to bring about the happily ever after. Sadly, happiness was nowhere to be found.

Wedding Day.

CHAPTER TWELVE
THE WORLD CLOSING IN

I will instruct you and teach you in the way you should go; I will
counsel you and watch over you.

—Psalm 32:8

To begin with, we argued about which apartment we should
choose. I wanted a moderately priced, small apartment. Gene
wanted a larger one with amenities that reflected the high rent. We
moved into a small place and purchased a brown, yellow, and
orange couch that clashed horribly with the royal blue carpet. This
apartment became the battleground for constant quarrels.

Our goals kept us grounded. Gene studied for his CPA
certification while he worked at an accounting firm. I worked as an
accounting clerk for the American Red Cross. We argued constantly
about money since our views and priorities in spending clashed.
Despite the heated fights, we stayed together. Our relationship

improved once Gene's CPA certification resulted in well-paying positions so that our finances were no longer an issue. Life became more peaceful, and we gradually adjusted to each other's different way of thinking.

That all changed again eighteen months later when we decided to have a baby. During our nine-month engagement, we'd focused on being in love. The topic of my retinal disease had been largely buried in the dreams we had for our future. Those dreams included having little ones running around and adding happiness to our life. One evening after we finished dinner at our favorite restaurant, Gene took my hand.

"Before we start a family, I think we should see a specialist," he said seriously. "We need to find out the possibilities of our kids inheriting RP."

I stared at him in silence. I dreaded the doctor's official confirmation that I would pass this disease on to our kids. But I knew Gene was right. I gave a slight nod. "I know."

We made the appointment. After the ophthalmologist finished his examination of my dilated eyes, he tapped his index finger on the table. "Janet, I don't have to tell you that your retinal disease can be passed on to your children. The fact is that each child will have a fifty-fifty chance of inheriting it." He paused before adding, "I think you should consider adoption."

A chill went through me. Adopt? Never have my own babies? I fought the urge to scream, "No, don't take that from me! Don't you understand? My deepest desire is to be a mom."

Gene turned to me. "We'll think about it, right?"

I nodded slowly, holding back my tears. As we left the ophthalmologist's office, Gene hugged me. "It's all going to be okay."

I rationalized that God would be the ultimate decision-maker. Once we arrived home, Gene and I dismissed the ophthalmologist's advice and made no effort to prevent conception. At Mass, I prayed silently, *God, if we are to have children, will You please protect them?*

A few months later, we were expecting our first baby. In due time, we gave birth to our first son Jason. Two years later, his younger brother Jeff came along. Eighteen months after that, our third son Joe completed the family.

As our family grew, so did Gene's income along with generous promotions at his St. Louis CPA firm. With joy overflowing, I thanked God for providing sufficient income for me to stay home and care for my babies. It was the 1970s, so this mindset contradicted the cry from the feminist movement that urged women to "live up to their potential" by following a career. I joined an organization committed to supporting stay-at-home moms in their important role by offering parenting classes and activities for their children.

One day after one of the board meetings, I was walking out with my youngest son Joe in my arms when the president of this organization stopped me. "Janet, would you consider being interviewed on TV to talk about our organization?"

I grinned. "Absolutely!"

That led to several radio and television interviews. In each one, I asserted our organizational position and emphasized that stay-at-home moms have a vital role in society as they are molding the leaders of tomorrow.

Joe on Mom's lap, Jeff on left and Jason on right.

Gene supported me in this effort. He was a very involved father. Even when his workload at the office was intense, he came home with enough energy to play with our sons. He read to them and showed them constant affection. No matter how busy I was keeping up with their antics and constant motion, Gene knew that caring for my three little J's was my dream come true.

Yet in this pleasant pattern of our life, I'd become too busy to realize something else was happening. In the end, it caught me by surprise and turned my world upside down.

One morning, Gene grabbed his car keys and headed for the door. Pausing to kiss me goodbye, he said, "I'll have to work late again tonight."

I gave him a big smile and wink. "I guess that promotion has its price, right?"

I understood that his new position was demanding. Though sometimes draining, my own job of caring all day for my little guys was pure delight for me. After changing their diapers, bathing them, reading bedtime stories, and tucking them in bed, I would head downstairs to pick up toys and fold laundry. Sometimes as I lay exhausted in bed, I thought of how much I missed Gene's company in the evenings. But I also relished all the blessings his hard work provided our family, so I was determined he'd never hear any complaining from me.

What a drastic contrast our life was here in the United States compared to the poverty I'd grown up with in Bolivia. Though at the beginning Gene and I had struggled financially, he'd done well at every position he'd held. We'd built a beautiful two-story home. We drove BMWs. We enjoyed family vacations at Disney World. It was all a dream come true for this Bolivian *chica*.

But one day with no warning, the consequences of my retinal disease ended our dream life. While my central vision remained clear, my peripheral vision began to close in. I could manage, I told myself over and over again. I masked my worry with the hectic routine that three active little ones demanded. My sons needed me, and driving the car was a vital part of my job description in caring for them.

But if ignoring the unwanted intruder didn't work, denial didn't either. Each time I got behind the wheel, my concentration was intense. I limited driving to daytime hours and only to necessary places. Doctor's appointments. School activities. Soccer practice. Grocery shopping. As weeks passed by, embarrassing moments made me cringe.

Our neighborhood gatherings also lost their attraction for me. The fun moments with other couples while all our kids played outside became a source of uneasiness. Most of the time I managed to navigate as I always had, but sometimes I would bump into one of them or miss a step which I quickly blamed on being clumsy. My neighbors teased me about backing the car into the mailbox at the end of the driveway. I covered my embarrassment with a fake smile, trying to blurt an excuse. But inside, I was mortified.

As with driving, my outward way to cope was to be extra careful. I walked slowly as I carried a tray of veggies into the kitchen. Christy, our hostess, gestured toward a table. "Just set your dish over here."

I set my tray on the table. But I didn't see the spoon sticking out of a Jell-O salad bowl. As I bumped it, clumps of red Jell-O flew across the table and onto the floor. Christy hurried over with a paper towel. "It's no big deal. Let me help you clean that."

What was a big deal was all the whispering from the other women. They didn't think I heard their murmured words of pity over my diminishing vision. I stayed positive on the outside, but inside I cried. After all, they were right. I was once a normal mom just like them. Now I was turning into a different person, a pitiful handicapped woman who could no longer do many things.

"Is there any transplant possible?" I heard one husband ask Gene. "Or medication she's taking?"

"No, there's nothing that can be done," Gene responded and immediately changed the subject.

Was my husband also resentful of this ugly eye condition that stained our happiness? I wanted to ask him in private moments. Instead, I focused on avoiding any more embarrassing incidents. This added to the tension gripping me each time I started the car. But what was the option? Not driving would be even more painful.

As I drove out of our subdivision, I turned my head from side to side more frequently to make sure the road was clear. I also avoided major highways and drove only in familiar areas. One bright morning, I packed my three sons, who ranged then from eighteen months to six years old, into their car seats in the back. Before climbing into the driver's seat, I looked into their three little faces. "Now, listen, boys. You all need to be really quiet so Mommy can drive. No fighting or whining, okay?"

They nodded, but they were soon engaged in their usual chatter, questions, and sometimes whining. I did my best to ignore the distraction from the back seat as I drove carefully toward the doctor's office where we had an appointment, making sure I stayed within the white lines. A few blocks from the doctor's office, I engaged my turn signal, looked to my left, then slowly and carefully proceeded to change lanes.

Suddenly, a loud scrape jolted me. To my shock, a car had been in the lane right beside me, and I hadn't seen it. My sons began to cry. Slamming to a halt, I fought back my own tears, knowing what had happened was my fault. The other driver hopped out of his car, ran over to me, and pounded on the driver's window.

"Are you crazy or something?" he shouted. "What's the matter with you? Open this door."

No apologies on my part eased his rage. The louder he screamed, the louder my sons cried. Driving slowly back home, I thanked God no one was hurt. But I chastised myself. I should have listened to that doctor who had warned me three years earlier. Those memories now flooded my mind.

It had been my twenty-seventh birthday. Along with gifts from Gene and my family, I'd received a disturbing letter from the ophthalmologist. A recent field vision test revealed a drastic narrowing of my side vision. The letter he'd mailed me concluded: "My professional recommendation is that you no longer operate any motor vehicle. Your limited field vision poses serious risks."

Determined not to lose my independence, I'd torn the letter up and told no one about the admonition. Since then, I'd been convincing myself that my central vision was just fine. Now, three years later, I knew I'd been wrong. Sideswiping that car was pushing me into a painful decision. While the thought of never driving again left me feeling defeated, I knew I couldn't bear it if I caused an accident that injured my little guys or hurt someone else.

Arriving back home, I pulled into the driveway. My hands trembled as I pressed the remote button to open the garage door.

Once I'd driven the car inside, I could no longer hold back my tears. I buried my face in my hands.

I can't do this anymore! I cried out silently. Then I took a deep breath, straightened up, and wiped away my tears. I couldn't let my sons see me upset. But the accident had made the choice for me. No more driving.

That evening as Gene and I sat at the kitchen counter, I let him know of my decision and the inevitable changes this would bring. "It's too hard to keep driving. Today I ran into a car in the lane next to me."

Gene immediately turned toward the boys, who played in the family room. "Are they okay? Are you okay?"

I nodded. "Thankfully, yes. But the side of the car is scratched pretty badly."

Standing up, Gene came over and put his arms around me. "I'll do the driving from now on."

At that moment, I felt secure and protected. But Gene couldn't guard me from the effects of the retinal disease that was growing to be a threatening monster. And sadly, I soon learned I wasn't the only one under attack by that monster.

CHAPTER THIRTEEN
SHATTERED DREAMS

You keep track of all my sorrows.

—Psalm 56:8

One spring morning, I sat on my unmade bed with a wrinkled tissue in hand. My head throbbed from crying all through a sleepless night. The sound of my neighbor's car pulling away down the street stirred envy. Only weeks earlier, I'd enjoyed the same independence. Now I'd lost it along with my self-esteem and my confidence. I could no longer drive. What else would I be unable to do for my family?

Cartoons playing on the TV downstairs brought me back to the moment. With cautious steps, I made my way to the top of the stairway. I paused long enough to find the banister before heading down. My three sons were playing rambunctiously in the family room. As I entered the kitchen, six-year-old Jason ran up to me, "Mommy, can I make the cereal?"

I hugged him and kissed the top of his head. "Sure, you can. You're the big brother."

He must have noticed I needed help. Perhaps he'd seen me when I struck my leg on the open dishwasher door. Or he'd heard me let out an "ouch!" when I inadvertently touched a hot pot on the stove. I clapped my hands to get the boys' attention. "TV off. It's breakfast time. Then you need to get dressed for school."

The boys have adjusted to Mom's blindness.

That morning routine often included one of my sons losing something. Jeff called out from his room, "Mom, I can't find my backpack."

With full sight, I would simply have looked for the backpack until I found it. Now I needed my sons' assistance. "Okay everybody, let's help Jeff find it."

When they ignored my request, I changed the wording. "Whoever finds the backpack will get a special treat when you get home from school."

That stirred up a flurry of three little boys rushing here and there. Finally, one of them found the lost item. This happened often, and the item was usually found right before the boys' ride pulled into the driveway.

Another game awaited them after school. Rather than reminding them over and over to change out of their school clothes, I made it a contest. "The first one to change into their play clothes gets to invite a friend over."

The three rushed upstairs to win the race. As the months passed, playing games became my way to have my sons help me compensate for what I couldn't do as effectively as before. When I dropped an item on the floor, my middle son Jeff would come from nowhere and place the item in my hands. "Here, Mommy."

Even at their ages, each showed me tenderness in their own way. And I cherished our method of working together. By now the oldest two, Jeff and Jason, were at school, and even the youngest, Joe, went to preschool part of the day. All of which made the house much quieter. I cherished the hours I spent alone at home with my youngest son. As Joe napped, I would stare down at him with eyes blurred by tears, memorizing the curly brown hair that framed his face and his long eyelashes resting on chubby cheeks. I'd done the same with Jeff's and Jason's faces, trying to engrave those images in my heart.

But in moments when the boys were all at school and I was completely alone, the battle inside me raged. Should I hold on to hope that someone would find a cure for my disease? Or should I prepare for the worst?

My parents fought a similar battle. Though they lived near us, I'd refrained from asking for their help because I knew they were facing their own issues. My father, from whom I'd inherited the RP gene, was also losing his sight. But unlike me, he insisted on driving even after running into a bus. Mom tried to support him while at the same time reason with him that it was time to stop driving. He became angry when anyone mentioned his eye condition and resented any kind of help.

In all of this, Mom continued to display her giving nature, patience, and unwavering affection toward my father as well as me. She called me often. "How are you, honey. I just made extra chicken. How about if I bring it over?"

"Don't worry about me, Mamita," I would reassure her. "I'm fine. The kids are doing great too."

But in truth, I wasn't fine. My heart ached for my mom and for my father who was facing the same decrease in his vision. Time was going by quickly, and this meant continued vision loss for both Father and me. By this point, I had only a sliver of vision left. I resolved to do my own research for anything or anyone who could give us hope.

I learned of an organization that funded research for a cure for retinitis pigmentosa. But they made it clear that even if a cure was a remote possibility, this would take years. I didn't have years or even months. Just a few weeks later, my tunnel vision had narrowed to the point that I was constantly running into objects, tripping over toys, missing steps, or misjudging the edge of the table.

Gene made no complaint as he helped clean up dishes that had crashed to the floor and other messes. But when he was at work, leaving me alone with our sons, I struggled. For the most part, I managed to get all tasks done, fix meals, clean, comfort the boys when they got hurt, discipline them when they fought, and monitor their play. But sometimes when distracted by their antics, I would move a bit too quickly. This led to striking my forehead on the edge of an open cabinet door. I held my breath from the pain as blood mixed with my tears. My main concern was always to keep my sons from seeing me upset or crying.

Gene witnessed enough of these incidents when he was home. In the beginning, he offered comforting words. As they occurred more often, this dwindled into a quick, "Are you okay?"

He shared nothing of his own fears or concerns. And since I was battling my own anguish, I never pressed him to open up. I kept going, holding on to hope, desperately trying to prove that he still had the same wife he'd married almost a decade earlier—healthy, active, and with a bubbly personality. We both played the pretend game well. Neither of us verbalized the horrific probability of my ultimate blindness.

One evening while Gene wrestled with our sons in the family room, I carried a basket of laundry downstairs. Even though I descended carefully, I missed the last step. I tumbled forward and slammed my head on the corner of a table. Immediately, a huge lump formed on the side of my head. Gene ran toward me. "What happened?"

I held my throbbing head. "I missed a step, that's all."

Gene handed me an ice pack, frustration tinging his voice. "That's it! You've got to see another ophthalmologist."

We did. Once in the ophthalmologist's office, I sat in the examination chair while he followed the same test procedure as previous ophthalmologists. "We'll do a field test, but I can already see the rapid deterioration." The ophthalmologist sat back in his chair. "You're already aware there is no cure, treatment, or surgery."

His words pierced my heart. I knew what he really meant was that my blindness was inevitable. He must have seen the horror on my face because he added quickly, "Don't worry. It may be a long time before you lose your sight completely. That said, the probability is that you eventually will. You need to be prepared."

I gripped the arm of the chair with all my might. No, he had to be wrong. Doctors make mistakes, and he might be making one too. Night blindness and lack of peripheral vision was one thing. But going completely blind just couldn't happen. Not to me. Not now.

As Gene and I drove home from the appointment, I turned to him. "This can't be right. The other doctor said nothing would happen until I'm at least sixty."

Gene gave a long sigh. "I don't know who to believe anymore."

I didn't either. I covered my fear of impending blindness by reassuring Gene, trying to avoid any added stress on him. But I decided to take action on my own. I wouldn't rest until I found even a slight possibility of halting the RP progression. I inquired with eye specialists in the United States, Cuba, and Europe. I learned of a procedure in Russia where they insert needles into the eyeballs. This had shown some small positive results, but the side effects included severe infections.

Next, I made an appointment with an acupuncturist. As I lay on a table, the acupuncturist thrust needles around my eye sockets and more into my hands and feet. The only result of those sessions was the pain I suffered from the needles.

Then I learned of a woman who ran an RP research lab in California. She claimed promising results. Since the trip to California and the treatment would be costly, I needed counsel. A friend directed me to a fortune teller. "She will tell you if this treatment will cure you or not."

I booked a fortune-telling session. The fortune teller made some absurd assertions and took my money. After a few more useless garbled ramblings, I left. Next was a visit to a New Age healer. She had me inhale some aromas, then ran her hand a few inches above my body. "I'm feeling your energy."

My own energy drained when she gave me the hefty bill. In my moments alone, I prayed desperately, *God, are you going to help me?* I would have done anything to receive a hint of hope from anyone. But no one offered it to me, not even God.

Thoughts of Abuelita kneeling on her bed praying for all the family's plights prompted me to do the same. As a Catholic, I'd been taught how to pray. Now I prayed longer, more often, and sometimes in tears. I also knew the doctrine, rituals, and memorized prayers. Confession had always been an uncomfortable task for me, but I did it anyway. A few devoted Catholic friends lit candles on my behalf, hoping to gain favors from the saints. I never failed in going to Holy Communion at Sunday Mass. I did it all and received nothing.

But what I did eventually receive from Gene turned my world upside down.

CHAPTER FOURTEEN
A BLIND SINGLE MOM

Then they cried to the LORD in their trouble and he saved them from their distress.

—Psalm 107:13

What I'd dreaded for so long finally happened. One cold winter morning, I woke up and turned my head from side to side, hoping to catch a glimpse of something, anything. I blinked and wiped my eyes. But it seemed as if a gray sheet covered everything around me.

Ever so cruel! That's how God seemed to me. He had His fingers on the dimmer switch of my sight. And despite my pleas to heal me, He'd turned that switch further and further down until there was nothing. No colors. No shadows. Only a gray veil. I gritted my teeth. *Why, God? Why me? Why now?*

I'd always believed God was good. Abuelita had taught us about God's mercy and compassion. But maybe He just extended it to others, not to me. The brief Bible readings during Mass relayed instances where Jesus had healed blind men. Perhaps they were deserving of His healing. But why wasn't I?

As Gene showered to get ready for work, I lay my head back on the pillow. How awful for my sons to live with a blind mom. I'd always wanted to give them the best. Now they would grow up pitifully deprived.

And Gene must feel terribly cheated. He'd married a healthy young woman able to achieve anything. Now less than a decade after we'd exchanged our vows at the altar, he was married to a blind woman. Though the affection between us had decreased and intimate moments were rare, he didn't complain. I assumed his silence meant he'd accepted our situation and would continue to support me and provide for our family.

And I committed to do my own part. That morning, I made my way to the master bathroom, opened the drawer, and pulled out my makeup case. I stared at it, but my brain registered no images. Out of habit, I glanced up toward the mirror, but I saw only a blank nothing. My hands shook, and my rage exploded. Hurling the makeup case against the wall, I leaned on the counter, sobbing away my horrible life.

"Mommy?" The plaintive question from my youngest son Joe, who was now three, startled me.

I wiped at my tears and faked a smile. "Hey, sweet baby, I'll be there in a minute."

He wasn't fooled. A moment later, I felt his little arms around my neck. "Mommy, are you crying?"

I hugged him tight. "Sometimes mommies cry too, but I'm okay. Actually, I'm better than okay. How about some yummy pancakes?"

I was determined to make my sons feel secure under my care. Even with no sight I managed all the household chores, though it often took me twice as long as previously. I figured out a way to cook by tasting, smelling, and creating my own recipes. Folding laundry became easier when I put one staple in the shirt label of my oldest, two staples in my second son's shirt, and none on my youngest. Running my fingertips across the label, I quickly identified to whom each shirt belonged.

Ironing also needed careful attention. I followed the cord leading to the handle to avoid accidently touching the hot metal. I cleaned the kitchen floor barefoot so my feet would reveal the spots I'd missed. My memory developed through memorizing phone numbers of friends and family. I called friends for rides or to inquire about the content in school notes I pulled from my sons' backpacks. Their activities provided a convenient distraction from the pain Gene and I were both carrying.

We had both become tacitly accustomed to our new way of navigating life together. When leaving the house, I held Gene's hand while he led me, telling me of any approaching steps or obstacles in the way. But mistakenly, we invited another obstacle into our lives. A friend and her daughters came to visit, bringing with them an exchange student, a young woman from Mexico.

My friend's daughters headed to the basement to play with our boys. The Mexican student quickly followed to monitor them. Sitting across the kitchen table from me, my friend sipped at a

Coke. "You know, our exchange student is amazing with kids. She's like a big sister to my girls."

I was immediately intrigued. I could certainly use some help. Even better if my sons had a big brother to play with. "How long is she staying with you?"

"For a year. You should try it. We love having exchange students."

Gene and I agreed to try it. That's how Ramon from Spain came to live with us. But though our sons looked at him as a fun big brother, it wasn't fun for me. He came from an affluent family and knew nothing about household chores. His presence simply meant more laundry for me, more lunches to fix, and more dishes to wash. The only redeeming factors were that Ramon did play with the boys and taught them a few words in Spanish.

Gene always tried to be home on time when our sons had Boy Scout events or soccer games to attend. But as a rule, he stayed quite late at the office. One fall evening, he walked into the house. Instead of greeting our sons as he usually did, he took my hand. "We need to go for a ride."

Looking over at our exchange student, he added in a serious tone, "Ramon, we'll be back in a little while. Please keep an eye on the boys. They can watch TV with you until we get back."

Gene walked me to the car and opened the door for me. I slipped into the passenger seat as he went around to the driver's side. Clueless about why he'd be taking me for an unscheduled ride this time of day, I clicked on my seat belt. He started the car, and we drove silently out of our neighborhood. Where we headed wasn't important. I just wanted to know what was on his mind.

"So, what's going on? Did something change at the office? You're not thinking of leaving that job, are you?"

"No, of course not!" Gene responded with a tone of annoyance. "Why would I leave when I just got a new promotion?"

He gave a long sigh before continuing. "What I want to tell you is that I've been confiding in someone."

I caught my breath, stunned at his words. "What is that supposed to mean?"

"Just that I've been talking to someone who works with me in the office."

I swallowed hard. "You mean a woman?"

I didn't want to hear the answer. If it was what I was thinking, it would tear me apart. His voice dropped to a low mumble. "What I'm trying to say is that I haven't been happy for a while. And I have someone else in my life."

Someone else? What? Why? When? Those thoughts raced through my head. Where had I been that I hadn't even seen a clue? How had I totally missed that our marriage was in such an awful state? Did Gene have plans to leave me? Was this woman going to be his main focus now while he abandoned me and our boys?

So many questions rumbled inside me, but the answers didn't matter anymore. He'd already admitted it. Now my own battle began. Should I ask for more details? Should I beg him to stop this illicit relationship? Should I explode in anger at his painful confession? I wanted him to see the pathetic man he'd become to seek another woman while I was facing the horror of my blindness.

In the end, my response was brief. "I'm feeling sick. I need to use a bathroom."

Pulling into a fast-food restaurant, Gene walked me inside. I entered the women's bathroom and groped around for a stall. There, I vomited, wishing I could get rid of my heartache in the same way. Moments later, Gene knocked on the door. "Are you okay?"

At that moment, I hated his voice, I hated his company, and I hated my life. Though I didn't want to be with him one minute longer, I had to step out and face him, a reminder of my physical and now emotional darkness.

The weeks that followed became a series of blurry hazes. I walked around empty and hollow, unable to sleep or eat. My world hung by a thread as if I were dangling from a tall bridge. As I clung to it, my fingers slowly slipped inch by inch toward the edge. And rather than coming to my rescue as I'd expected, my husband had inadvertently stomped my fingers with all his might, leaving me to drop into a dark tunnel of desperation. He'd found happiness while I'd found despair.

But despite the anguishing heartache, I determined that caring for my sons would always be my greatest passion, something I could hold on to even if it meant ending up a blind single mom. I spent silent moments reviewing over and over again the years Gene and I had spent together. How had I missed the signs that Gene was so unhappy? How could I have allowed my blindness to tear our marriage apart?

As I fell asleep alone at night, regret, sorrow, blame, and rejection hovered over me like dark clouds in my storm. Each day I expected Gene to pack his bags and leave, but he didn't. He still came home at night, bringing his cold demeanor with him. We both agreed to seek counseling. But after a few sessions, the advice from our counselor was that we should get out of a relationship that wasn't working. Gene was still attentive to our sons and extended cordial but indifferent remarks toward me. Neither of us expected the dramatic change ahead of us.

Chapter Fifteen
New Vision

He guides the humble in what is right and teaches them his way.
—Psalm 25:9

The beautiful landscape adorning the front of our house now masked the ugliness inside. No one could have suspected the turmoil within its walls, nor did my parents suspect the rejection and anguish I was carrying. My positive, optimistic personality was gone, but they probably assumed it was my blindness that had caused this change.

One morning I ran my fingertips across the kitchen counter to find the lunch boxes for Jason and Jeff that I'd prepared the night before. "Here you go guys. Take your lunch and hurry. Andy's mom will be here any minute to pick you up."

I hadn't even showered or brushed my hair yet. Getting my boys ready for school took all my energy and focus. The doorbell rang, and

Jason opened it. I heard Andy's mom Sue as she entered the kitchen. She'd become a good friend in whom I confided. She gave me a hug.

"I'm a little early. I just wanted to make sure you're okay." She pulled back before asking, "Are you?"

I fought the urge to sob on her shoulder and spill out the devastation searing me inside. Instead, I swallowed the lump in my throat and nodded. "I'm just trying to get used to this new way of life. It's not easy, but it's okay."

Sue squeezed my hands. "I just can't imagine what you're going through."

She was right. Few could imagine being totally blind and facing marital infidelity. Instead of a "happily ever after," my life seemed to have become a story with a pitifully unhappy ending.

That evening, Sue called me. "Listen, I'm not sure if you'd be interested, but my church is having a healing service tonight. I can pick you up if you'd like to go."

Had I received that invitation before my blindness, I would have refused. A true Catholic doesn't visit a Protestant church. But those Catholic rules went out the window when Sue mentioned the word "healing." Since God hadn't heard me when I prayed inside a Catholic church, maybe He'd hear me at a Protestant church. But I was cautious about getting my hopes up too high. I feared this would just set me up for another disappointment.

"Okay, I'll go with you," I finally said. "Thanks."

Meanwhile, our exchange student's stay had been cut short. Ramon's parents sent airline tickets for him to visit family friends. Although his departure was only a few days away, he agreed to stay with our sons that evening. Sue picked me up. Once in the church parking lot, I took her arm. We went inside and sat in a pew.

As we settled in, I reached into my purse to find my tissues. So often now my tears came unexpectedly, and this time I couldn't control them. Silently, I pleaded, *God will You hear me this time? Will You heal me? Will You heal my marriage? My life?*

The service began with singing. Then the pastor addressed the congregation and went on to Bible teaching. He read verse after verse. Some were slightly familiar. But unlike a Catholic Mass, the preacher expanded on each verse, analyzed them, and drew life applications. They all made sense and were refreshingly encouraging. Nearly every verse he read mentioned God's healing power, His faithfulness and His pure love.

Pure love? What was wrong with me? I didn't feel that love. Instead, I'd experienced God's hand seemingly punishing me. In my mind, God had undeservingly chastised me with painfully unfair adversity. As soft music played in the background, the preacher invited those who needed prayer for healing to come to the front.

"Do you want to go?" Sue whispered.

I nodded, and we headed down the aisle. Two women placed their hands on me. Their fervent prayers for my healing moved me. In that instant, I dared to believe God would perform a miracle. But when they'd finished and Sue and I returned to our pew, I still saw nothing. No change. No healing. Once again, my heart cried out in desperation. *Show me what I'm doing wrong, Lord. Where are your answers?*

That night as usual, Gene didn't come home to spend time with our sons before they went to bed. Once they were asleep, I was alone with my thoughts. Images of Gene with another woman instead of working late, as he'd always claimed, mortified me. I lay awake, trying to replace those images with the encouraging Bible verses the preacher had read. I wished I could access them. But even if I could see, reading the Bible would be as odd to me as flying an airplane.

To me, this last episode with Gene simply emphasized that I was too unlovable, unworthy, and undeserving to be healed. Undeserving of Gene's love and undeserving of God's love. And yet the preacher that evening had repeatedly spoken of God's unfailing love. The world had failed me, and so had my once healthy body. Did I even dare believe God would not? Maybe God wasn't cruel, but compassionate after all.

Restlessness kept me awake, and I sensed a new hunger in me. Not for Gene. Not for our marriage. Not even for my sight. I yearned for something I couldn't explain. I called Sue. "If it's okay with you, let me know when you're going back to your church. I'd like to come with you."

Sue picked me up for the next service. Once again, I sat on the pew beside her. This time instead of tears, reassurance filled me. As the preacher read Bible verses, they filtered into my heart, depositing comforting peace. I hung on to every word. But the verse that most impacted my heart came from words spoken directly by Jesus Himself. "Seek first the kingdom of God and His righteousness and all these things shall be added unto you."

I held my breath as those words echoed through the church sanctuary. God was speaking directly to me. He knew what I'd been seeking with all my might. To see again. To have my marriage back. To be normal like before. Those had been my top desires. Nothing else mattered.

Now I realized that my priorities had been upside down. *Seek Me first*, God was saying to me. I lowered my head, and tears flowed. But this time my tears carried gratitude, regret, clarity, and hope all at the same time. In my heart, I cried out, *Lord, how do I seek You? Show me, God. I'm dying inside.*

Though my outward vision was gone, I saw clearly in my mind's eye God pointing to the path before me. Desperation gripped me again. But this time I was desperate to know more. To tap once again into that wonderfully strange peace I'd felt. I leaned toward Sue. "Where do I find that verse?"

"It's Matthew 6:33," she responded. "From the Sermon on the Mount. I'll help you find it."

Not only did she help me find it, but she found a complete Bible in audio. Those two cases filled with cassettes seemed intimidating at first. Every chance I had while my sons were at school, sleeping, or playing outside, I grabbed a pair of earphones and listened to different books of the Bible, sometimes in the Old Testament, sometimes in the New. After weeks and weeks of listening, I became a master at rewinding the portions that particularly touched me. I memorized passages so I could repeat them through the day.

One afternoon while I sat at our glass patio table, I slipped my earphones on and looked upward. The sun caressed my face and arms, but the sky above me was a dark blank instead of the white puffy clouds dotting blue skies I'd enjoyed when I was sighted. As I listened to a cassette from the book of Psalms, I pondered about how dark my surroundings had become. Just then a verse jumped out at me:

Your Word is a lamp to my feet and a light for my path.

—Psalm 119:105

I rewound that verse again and again until I'd engraved it in my heart. With one swift move, I slipped the earphones off, buried my face in my hands, and sobbed. *Thank You, God, thank You for speaking to me. Your Word is all the light I need. You will lead me. You will guide me.*

That scenario of listening, then understanding, and finally in tears, thanking God for His promises soon became a regular routine for me. Each day and week, I embraced new promises from God. He promised that He had plans for my life that weren't to hurt me but to prosper me and to give me hope and a future (Jeremiah 29:11). He reassured me His love would never fail me, that His timing is perfect, and His healing is certain. No more stumbling on the terrain of painful disappointments. Instead, I would walk firmly on God's promises.

One afternoon, I folded laundry in the family room while listening to a TV broadcast of *The 700 Club*, a Christian program. Sheila Walsh was the host and offered a phone number to anyone who needed prayers. By then I memorized phone numbers easily. Heading over to the phone, I called the number. A sweet, soft female voice answered.

"Have you invited Jesus to be your personal Savior?" the woman asked me.

Invite Jesus? No, I hadn't. I didn't even know I needed to do this. But if it had to do with obeying God's Word and with God's Son Jesus, who performed miracles and loved me so much that He'd died for me, then of course I wanted to invite Him into my life.

I did so right then and there. I made Jesus the Lord of all. My blindness. My marriage. My life. What happened next shocked even me.

CHAPTER SIXTEEN
TURNING POINT

Who is it that overcomes the world? Only he who believes that Jesus is the Son of God.

—1 John 5:5

As expected, losing my sight caused my hearing to become more acute. I placed a turkey and cheese sandwich in front of my oldest son Jason one afternoon. His munching caught my attention. "Close your mouth when you chew, honey."

"I forgot," he said. "You know, you're the only mom in the world who can fix stuff with no lights on."

I kissed his cheek. "Pretty cool, huh?"

I loved that my sons saw the positive side of their mom's blindness. Joe, the youngest, had his own observations. One day while I made my way down the steps to the basement, I heard Joe and his friends chattering.

"You know," Joe said, "my mom has eyes at the end of her fingers."

I grinned. That's how it must seem to him. I navigated by running my fingers across countertops to find items and on furniture to give me a point of reference. My middle son Jeff also found the positive side of my blindness.

"Mom, can you come to my class?" he asked. "My teacher said she wants you to tell us how you do things when you can't see."

I took turns visiting their classrooms. Their teachers found it valuable for their students to learn how many things a person can do even without sight.

While my sons were in school, I concentrated on learning from Christian programs. *Focus on the Family* shared insights I applied in my role as a mom. One day as I emptied the dishwasher, I listened to Bible teacher Charles Stanley saying, "You can follow God's plans and live a life rich and abundant. Or you can follow your own plans and live a life empty and anxious."

I had lived the latter. How delightful it was now to be learning God's path for my new life with confidence, trust, and wisdom. Just then, the doorbell interrupted my learning session. I walked over to the door. "Who is it?"

"It's me."

I immediately recognized Christy's voice. She lived across the street and had become my faithful friend. She helped me pick up toys, shared recipes with me, and even invited me to shopping trips. Opening the door, I motioned for her to come in. "Promise me we'll just visit this time. No cleaning."

"Okay, okay," she said. "I just don't want you tripping over the kids' toys."

Christy sat down at the kitchen counter. I moved toward the cabinet. "Want some tea?"

"I can get it," she said.

"Nope, I'll do it." I winked at her. "You can trust me."

Christy took a cup and teaspoon from me. "Something's going on. You seem pretty happy. And your sense of humor is back."

"Wanna know the secret?"

"I'm ready," she chuckled. "What have you been up to?"

Running my fingertips to the end of the counter, I tapped at the case of cassettes. "This is what's going on. Do you know what these are?"

"Hmm! Are you listening to music?" she hazarded a guess.

"You could say that. It's music for my heart." I gave her a big smile. "These are cassettes with the Bible on them. It's a crazy thing. I just can't get enough of it."

"I've never really tried to read the Bible myself," Christy said. "Way too complicated for me."

Sitting across from her, I stirred honey into my tea. "Exactly how I felt. But when your heart is desperate, well, let's just say that all I'm hearing makes perfect sense. For the first time, I know God is actually speaking to me."

"So does Gene read the Bible, too?"

I inhaled deeply. "Gene's on a different level right now. I'm not sure he'd be interested."

I was relieved when Christy didn't ask any further questions about my husband. She had no idea of our crumbling marriage. I poured my heart out to God, my Lord and divine confidant, but not to friends, not even Christy.

She spoke up. "Guess what. I'm having a Mary Kay party, and you're coming."

I gave her an "are you kidding?" look. "What would I do with makeup?"

"You never know," she said in a sing-song tone.

I accepted her invitation. That day, I sat with five other women around Christy's dining room table. The Mary Kay representative explained the steps for proper skin care and ways to apply eye shadow and eyeliner.

"Hey girlfriend, give me that eyeliner," I said. "Let me see what I can do."

I was joking, but they put the pencil in my hand. I carefully placed the tip at the base of my eyelashes and drew the line across. I opened my eyes. "What do you think?"

"Are you kidding, Janet?" one of them said. "How did you do that so well? You can't even—"

I interrupted her with a big smile. "Careful! Jealousy is an ugly thing. Anyone got an eyelash curler?"

Someone placed one in my hand. I raised it to my eyes. "Any bets I can do this?"

They all laughed. Then there was perfect silence as I pressed the curler on my eyelashes. I blinked, showing them off. "Voila!"

Applying mascara and eye shadow was simple since I could use the brush as a guide. The fun and laughing with girlfriends encouraged me. But what hung over me were the unresolved issues with Gene. I no longer wished he would reach for me. I didn't want what he used to offer. Not his kisses, his embrace, or his whispers that he was crazy about me. Not from a confused man too weak to resist immoral desires.

As I lay on my side of our king-size bed, his voice interrupted my thoughts. "Can we talk?"

I turned away from him. "Yes, but not now. I'm way too tired. Maybe tomorrow."

The next evening after my sons and I finished dinner, they ran outside to play. I cleared the table and grabbed the washcloth to wipe the counter. The sound of the garage door opening startled me. It was too early for Gene to be home, but to my surprise, he stepped into the kitchen.

"I'm home," he said in a somber tone.

I continued my cleaning. "I know."

"Can we talk now?"

I tossed the washcloth in the sink and grabbed a towel. As I dried my hands, I leaned on the counter, facing in his direction. "I'm listening."

"We have to make a decision."

"I made mine," I said. "If you remember, I didn't force you to marry me. And I won't force you to stay with me either." I took a long breath before continuing. "If you choose to leave, the boys and I will be fine. I now have someone in my life I can trust. Someone who won't leave me or betray me. His name is Jesus. I'll be okay. You're free to go."

"Are you trying to get rid of me?" Gene demanded.

I nodded. "I'm trying to get rid of the man you've become. But I would welcome the man you used to be."

113

Gene said nothing. Moments later, his steps faded as he went down the hall. A few days later, he headed downstairs into the kitchen.

"I'm making the boys breakfast," he announced.

"You're not going to work?" I asked, puzzled.

He pulled bowls from the cabinet. "I'm not going to work because I put in my resignation."

I was speechless. Why would Gene leave such a great position? What would we do for income? Did he have another job lined up somewhere else?

Coming towards me, Gene took my hands. "I'm leaving all that behind. I'm not going back to the company, to her, or anything else. If you'll have me, I'm making the commitment to stay here with you and with our sons. I want nothing more."

Should I hug his neck? Or hold off for wisdom before responding?

Chapter Seventeen
Delicious Restoration

I will restore to you the years that the swarming locust has eaten...
You shall eat in plenty and be satisfied, and praise the name of the
Lord your God, who has dealt wondrously with you.

—Joel 2:25-26

I tried to digest what Gene had just announced as I stared in his
direction. "Let me understand. You just got that promotion, but
you're now quitting your job?"

"Yes, that's precisely what I said." Gene's voice projected
confidence. "I want to prove to you that nothing else matters but
you and the boys."

The old me—insecure, empty, and hungry for approval—would
have reached for him and thanked him profusely for committing to
love me again. But during the months that had passed since he'd first
confessed his infidelity, my focus had changed. My new life with

Jesus at the center had transformed me. I wasn't that vulnerable, broken young woman anymore. God's Word infused me with confidence and security. My blindness didn't define who I was. God did. I was His daughter, possessing significance, purpose, and worth.

When I'd originally entered into marriage, I'd done so foolishly believing Gene could make me whole. How deceived I'd been in thinking he was the source of my joy, happiness, and security. I'd been equally wrong in allowing Gene's infidelity and rejection to rob me of that sense of worth. But now I walked on solid ground. My daily habit of internalizing God's Word had opened the eyes of my heart. This in turn gave me holy boldness and wisdom.

I was about to respond to Gene's announcement of renewed devotion to our family when our sons' voices from the backyard caught my attention. They reminded me that the boys needed their father. Just as important, I needed to be strong enough to set non-negotiable boundaries.

Gene squeezed my hands. "Will you take me back?"

His voice was soft and seemingly genuine. But I released my hands from his. "You and I will never make it together on our own. If we're going to move forward, we have to put Jesus at the center of our marriage."

Gene lifted my hand and kissed it. "That's reasonable. I agree."

I gave a faint smile. "And we have to begin praying together."

He hugged me. "I promise we will."

I couldn't trust his promises. Not yet. Instead, I trusted in God's Word, which assured me that God would add "all these things" if I continued to seek Him first (Matthew 6:33). Listening to the Bible and receiving God's Word had become second nature to me. Entering into that routine with Gene turned out to be awkward. Going from reciting memorized prayers, as was the custom in the Catholic Church, to reading the Bible together was new and unfamiliar for us. But we persevered. We still attended Sunday Mass as a family. Gene also supported my participation in an evening Bible study, and he agreed to listen to Christian teachings during the week with me.

One evening as we drove home, we were listening to *Focus on the Family* on the radio. The host announced a *Promise Keepers* conference, which invited men to commit themselves to the vows they'd made to God and to their marriages.

Gene patted my hand. "I think I want to attend. What do you think?"

My heart leapt at his words. I turned to him with a huge smile. "Absolutely."

At that conference together with hundreds of other men, Gene gave his heart to Jesus. The same Bible verse that had turned my life around came to mind as Gene told me of his decision. God had declared His promise that if we seek Him first, all these things would be added unto us. Gene's salvation was an addition that highlighted God's faithfulness.

But now my own faithfulness to God's Word would be tested. I had to obey God's instruction to forgive. My heart was empty of resentment, vengeance, or anger, and I was ready and willing to offer Gene genuine, complete forgiveness. I committed to let go and move forward with the new man Gene had become.

A few weeks later, a headhunter called Gene with an attractive offer for a position in a company closer to our home. It was a perfect fit for him. Perfect for me too as I could continue being a blind, but immensely happy stay-at-home mom to our sons.

I'd developed a routine that worked. When I stepped into the kitchen, I found no need to follow recipes. Instead, I invented my own using only healthy ingredients. When I served my homemade spaghetti, our sons practically licked their plate. The specific way I marked boxes in the pantry, separated cans, and constantly tasted and added spices paid off. I relished in my accomplishments, not only in cooking but cleaning and keeping up with the boys' constant motion.

Gene was consistent in coming home in the evenings. We would eat a quick dinner, then head out to take our sons to sports activities or Cub Scouts. He played catch with our boys in the backyard. Grocery shopping and yardwork kept his weekends busy. Life became beautifully active as Gene and I found time to attend Marriage Encounter conferences, Bible studies, and small group meetings at church. Friends never failed to provide rides for me to attend prayer sessions.

But while all had seemed to fall into place, our mutual concern about our sons inheriting my retinal disease still hovered in the background. One day as we drove home after one of our marriage sessions, I turned to Gene. "I've been thinking that the boys are old enough to have their eyes tested."

"I know." Sadness filled Gene's voice. "Even if there's nothing we can do about it, we need to know."

We took the boys to the best ophthalmologist in St. Louis. All three handled the uncomfortable tests well. Our two younger boys' retinas seemed clear of any sign of RP, but Jason showed some inconclusive signs. When I heard the news, I fought grief with the weapon of God's promise. The same promise He'd given me that God would be Jason's guide and healer. Instead of worrying, I vowed to place Jason in God's hands.

One evening when I came home from a prayer session, I walked into the family room, scooped up my youngest son Joe in my arms, and twirled him around in the air. "Hey sweet boy, were you good for Daddy?"

He giggled. Putting him down, I extended my hand toward Jason and Jeff. "C'mon, you two. Who wants to put the bubbles in the tub first?"

"Me!" all three chimed.

I took Jeff's hand. "Then it's upstairs for all of you. Bath time first, then Bible stories."

"Need help?" Gene asked.

He knew I managed most tasks for the family with ease, and he didn't push when I responded, "Nope. I've got this."

Later in the silence of the night, gratitude overflowed in me. I pondered on the true, trustworthy Word of God when He promised to heal and restore. God had healed something far more important than my eyesight. He'd given me wisdom to focus beyond my circumstances to change my priorities. He'd shown me the beauty of a life free from fear and insecurities. I relished in seeing my world with appreciation for what I still had rather than lamenting what I'd lost.

Chapter Eighteen
A New Chapter

Delight yourself in the LORD and he will give you the desires of your heart.

—Psalm 37:4

I came to realize that the only two things I'd really lost were my longing to be sighted again and my desire for what life used to be. Instead, I now looked forward each day to the future. As I listened to Bible verses about God's plan and purpose for His children, I wondered what His plans would be for me. What would I do with my life once my boys left home and started their own families? Being blind, what work could I do?

I'd earned my Bachelor of Business Administration degree, but without eyesight, working in an office setting was unrealistic. What I worked on instead was to embrace God's promises about fulfilling our desires. God's Word said, *Delight yourself in the Lord, and He will give you the desires of your heart* (Psalm 37:4). I believed that what God promised, He would bring about. I just didn't know how that would come to be.

One afternoon, an acquaintance called asking a favor. She had cassettes that were in Spanish, and she wanted me to translate them for her into English. A piece of cake since Spanish was my native language. When I finished, I called her. She picked up the cassette tapes. After listening to the translation, she contacted me. "I've had other material translated before. But no one else has done such a great job."

I grinned. "Do you have any more?"

"Not at the moment. But if I get more, you'll be my first choice. Did you ever consider working as a Spanish interpreter?"

An interpreter? No way! What I'd done for her required little effort. I'd simply listened to the material in Spanish, then recorded it in English. But spoken interpretation would require skills I didn't have. Then I remembered what God had said to Joshua when He called Joshua to lead the Israelites into the Promised Land after the death of Moses:

Have I not commanded you? Be strong and courageous. Do not be afraid; do not be discouraged, for the Lord your God will be with you wherever you go. (Joshua 1:9)

Joshua's task was to be strong and courageous. God's promise was to be with Joshua wherever he went. If God did that for Joshua, I knew He would do that for me as well. Tapping into that holy boldness, I called the largest interpreting company in St. Louis where we lived.

"Yes, we're hiring Spanish interpreters," the receptionist said. "All you have to do is take a test to assess your skills."

A test? I immediately regretted not having learned braille. Some months prior, Peggy, a teacher from services for the blind who was also blind herself, had come to our house. She'd placed a big book of braille before me. "Let's begin with the alphabet."

I did my best and learned all the braille letters. But the more we explored the variation of dots and their positions, the less enthusiasm I felt. Closing the book, I turned to Peggy. "Can we forget about this braille stuff and become friends instead?"

She chuckled. "Sure."

That was the end of my braille exposure. Now that I was facing a test for the interpreting company, braille might have come in handy.

"It's an oral test," the receptionist mentioned quickly, "And we have an opening tomorrow if you'd be interested."

The second I heard the word "oral," I was convinced. "I'll be there."

My sweet mom drove me to the interview. As we walked into the building, my muscles tightened a bit. But like with Joshua, I knew God would be with me. I had nothing to worry about. Nothing to lose or fear. I relaxed enough to concentrate intently on each portion read to me. Without much trouble, I rendered its interpretation.

The next day, the receptionist called. "I wanted to give you the results of your test."

Gulp! "Did I pass?"

"You sure did. Your score is impressive. We'd like to send you to the Immigration and Naturalization court for your first assignment tomorrow."

I resisted leaping in the air. Although this was a daring challenge for me, God was clearly opening the door to this new adventure, and I was eager to get started. When Gene came home, I gave him the good news.

He hugged me tightly. "I'm so proud of you. And the court building is only blocks from my office. I'll drop you off."

By then, I'd received mobility training to walk with the white cane that marked me as lacking sight. I called it the cane that nudged me from pride to humility. Initially, I resisted that stage of blindness. Using the white cane was admitting to the world that I belonged to a sad demographic designated "blind." But once the stench of pride faded away, humility and gratitude took its place.

That morning our sons sat at the kitchen table, munching on their cereal. I reached for Jason's bowl. "Are you done, honey? We need to hurry a little. Mommy has to go and interpret."

"I'm done." Jason stood up from the table. "But what's interpret?"

I handed him his bookbag. "When someone doesn't speak English, they need an interpreter to tell them in Spanish what is being said."

As I carried empty bowls toward the sink, Gene took them from me. "I got these. You can finish getting ready while I drop them off at school."

I headed to the stairway. "Got to find something to wear."

Gene ran the water in the sink. "You'll dazzle them, baby, no matter what you wear."

I hurried upstairs and stepped into the bathroom. No need to turn on the light or use a mirror either. I pulled out my makeup case. First the eye shadow, then the eyelash curler, eyeliner, and last, the mascara. The process had become easy.

I'd manicured my nails the night before, and I was now ready to choose the right outfit to wear. Once in my closet, I ran my hand across the hanging items to make my selection. At the time I purchased each item, I asked for a description. I made sure to memorize the texture, neckline, buttons, color, and any other unique characteristic. With this information in my head, I needed no help in selecting my outfits. The same process made my jewelry and shoe selection quick and easy. That morning, I chose a gray suit with black piping and black pumps.

Gene and I drove to the court building in downtown St. Louis. He walked me inside, and I settled in a chair outside the courtroom, my purse on my lap and the white cane beside me. Alone in that unfamiliar setting, one by one, thoughts of apprehension and doubt attacked me. Just the day before, I'd been folding laundry. Now I was about to enter a real-life courtroom. I swallowed hard and began to analyze the uncomfortable reality.

What happened next should be an entry in the book of miracles.

CHAPTER NINETEEN
OPEN DOORS

And we know that in all things God works for the good of those
who love him, who have been called according to his purpose.

—Romans 8:28

I fidgeted in my seat outside the courtroom. What was I doing here?
I knew nothing about interpreting, legal terminology, or even what
went on in such proceedings. Had cell phones been available back
then, I would have grabbed one and called Gene to pick me up.

Instead, I was stuck facing an intimidating scenario. What
would I do if I heard an unfamiliar word? What if I make a fool of
myself in that courtroom in front of the attorneys and the judge?
The more I thought about my sorry predicament, the more my
stomach churned. No matter my discomfort, I had no way out.

Then something changed. A Bible verse I'd learned about our
thoughts popped into my head. *Whatever is right, whatever pure, if*

anything is excellent or praiseworthy, think about such things, and the God of peace will be with you. At the time, I couldn't remember the exact wording or Bible reference (Philippians 4:8-9). But God whispered His reassurance to me through those words.

New thoughts replaced my fears and worries. I prayed silently. *Lord, your Word is what is excellent. Your promises are praiseworthy. I trust in You, and I know You will do for me what I can't do for myself.*

"Ms. Eckles?" The court clerk's voice interrupted my silent prayers. "We're ready for you."

Looping my purse on my shoulder, I grabbed my cane. "May I hold your arm for guidance?"

"No problem." His arm brushed lightly against mine. "Here you go."

We entered into the hush of the courtroom. With a subtle hand movement extending forward, I found the back of my chair and settled in it. Moments later, I heard voices identifying where the other participants were each sitting. Sweat formed on my forehead when I realized I was the only woman there.

I trust you, Lord, I prayed quietly.

The session began. No one indicated when I should begin interpreting. When the judge asked me to raise my right hand and take the interpreter's oath, I assumed that was my clue. From that point on, I repeated in Spanish anything the attorneys said in English. When the respondent spoke in Spanish, I repeated it in English. As the session continued, my tension increased.

Then mercy came. The judge slammed down his gavel. "We'll take a ten-minute recess."

I was ready to hug the judge for that break in my torture. But my relief was short-lived. The judge spoke again with the authority of a stern sergeant. "Madam interpreter, please approach the bench."

I swallowed hard as I grabbed my cane. When I stood up, the bailiff took my arm and guided me toward the judge's bench. I tried to sound professional, but my voice still trembled. "Your Honor?"

The judge's voice turned unexpectedly gentle. "I just want you to know that I am also bilingual in English and Spanish. I appreciate your level of accuracy and professionalism."

Everything in me wanted to jump up in the air and shout, "Yay, God!" Instead, I lowered my head. "Thank you, Your Honor."

After the session, a tap on my shoulder startled me. Placing a business card in my hand, a man said, "Here. Please call my office. I'd like to have your contact information for other hearings."

Hearings? So that's what the session was called. I grinned. "Thank you so much."

I finally relaxed, my heart overflowing with gratitude for God's goodness. Gene picked me up. As we headed home, he asked, "How did it go? Tell me all about it."

"I almost died at the beginning, but God was so good to me. I'm baffled. The judge said I did okay."

"Baby, you were more than okay. I know you." Gene squeezed my hand. "There's nothing you can't do. And whatever you do, you do it excellently."

Gene's way of expressing himself had always impressed me. But it was his support that touched me. One year had now passed since I'd lost my sight. What I'd gained was creativity to find different ways to manage tasks. I couldn't write information so I learned to rely on my memory. I developed a habit of storing in my head important dates for appointments and lists of phone numbers. Our sons' school. Neighbors. Relatives. The local pharmacy and doctors' offices. Even our local pizza place.

That practice made memorizing legal terminology and their equivalent in Spanish a simple task. I had another advantage. My concentration with no visual distractions kept my accuracy level high. I was also diligent in practicing every chance I got. Whenever the TV was on or we listened to radio programs, I would interpret mentally everything that was said.

I also asked Gene to check the bilingual dictionary for certain unfamiliar terms so I could add them to the list I'd filed in my memory. This method plus the desire to excel soon helped me to master the skill of interpreting. I received letters of commendations from judges and attorneys encouraging me to accept more assignments.

Looking back, I saw how God had given me the desire of my heart to be productive during my sons' school hours. My limited expectations had included perhaps a hobby or participation in a worthwhile organization. Instead, God had opened doors wide to wow me and emphasize His promise: *All these things shall be added unto you* (Matthew 6:33).

One evening while I cleaned the kitchen, Gene came home from work and placed his computer case on the counter. "How was your interpreting today?"

"The session went well. But the cab took forever. I hate not being here when the kids get home."

"They'll be okay. It's not a daily occurrence."

"I know." I finished wiping the counter. "But I'm thinking maybe I should just put off this interpreting stuff until they grow up a little."

Gene grabbed the washcloth from my hands and tossed it into the sink. Then he lifted my chin with his fingertips. "Listen. What is it you always tell me? To pray about it, right?"

I smiled widely and nodded. Not only because he was right but because he wasn't shy in showing his conviction to seek God first. One day as I listened to Bible verses, God reminded me that He knows our needs even before we speak them. During one of my assignments, I walked into the courtroom.

"Janet, let me help you," a fellow interpreter said, steering me to my seat.

I recognized his voice. "Thanks, Mike."

Mike sat beside me. "Have you heard about the company that offers interpreting over the phone?"

"Over the phone? I'm not even sure how that would work."

"I know, I thought it was crazy at first too," he said. "But it's a real business. You can work from home and do all your interpreting over the phone."

I grinned. "How amazing! Really?"

Mike gave me the necessary information. Once I got home that evening, I got a number for the company from the phone directory and called them. With as much professionalism as I could muster, I listed my experience in the courtroom. "I'd like to apply for a Spanish interpreter's position."

"Absolutely!" The enthusiasm in her voice encouraged me.

Since we lived in St. Louis and the company was in California, the entire job interview was done on the phone. Gene helped me fill out the application, then the company interviewed me a second time. After testing my abilities, they offered me the job on the spot. It was one more dream come true. I could interpret on the phone and never leave home. So much excitement bubbled up in me that I almost broke out into a cha-cha-cha. *Thank you, Lord!*

One thing I'd failed to mention to my new employers was my blindness. The reason was logical and quite reasonable—they never asked.

I was to begin taking calls in just two days. As I pondered this amazing new adventure, I fell into the thinking tank again. Interpreting in the courtroom was done simultaneously, which didn't require taking notes. But interpreting on the phone would require writing down information. From those notes, I would then interpret to the other person also on the phone. Without sight, writing anything down would be impossible.

That obstacle became the needle that deflated my balloon. Should I call the company back and confess I was blind? Or should I trust that God had an answer for this predicament? After all, the Bible says that some things may be impossible for man, but with God all things are possible (Matthew 19:26).

I once again turned to prayer, this time with a little more boldness. *Lord, I'm facing a truly impossible task. I'm asking for a miracle. Either give me my sight back today, or You'll have to show me how to do this.*

While I didn't doubt God would do something, my heart was racing as the first call came in. I used my most courteous voice, and I rendered the interpretation quickly. That became my way of making sure the speaker didn't talk too long, which would have made it more difficult for me to remember everything said. I did the same with both the English and Spanish speaker. The more calls I took, the easier it became to follow that pattern.

I interpreted while my sons were at school. When they got home, no one else greeted them but me. My heart smiled. This job was perfect for me in every way. And each new day reminded me again that God's Word is truly a lamp unto our feet and a light for our path (Psalm 119:105). He guided me step by step. His light shone as he took me from pain to peace, from doubt to trust, and from fear to faith. I remembered how I'd feared that my sons would grow up deprived. In this new season, my faith became firm to believe God would not allow that to happen.

One afternoon when Joe was about six years old, he came into my office. "Mom, you do more than all my friends' moms. You have a job. You clean the house. You cook for us. And you can't even see. That's amazing."

"Come here, sweet boy." Grabbing him, I hugged my son tight. "Who loves you more than anyone else in the whole wide world?"

He wiggled in my arms. "Jesus."

My family adjusted beautifully to the new routine of me working. When they saw the door to my office closed, they knew they needed to be extra quiet. My breaks and lunch hour allowed me to organize our home, fix quick meals, and monitor their activities. I followed that routine each day and looked forward to my shift since the various interpretation sessions were always interesting if occasionally a challenge.

I'd have been far more stressed had I known the monitoring process the company implemented. Without giving the interpreters any advance warning, our calls were being monitored. Subsequent feedback included ratings for every detail of our interpreting performance. Because of God's grace, my reviews included praises that humbled me with gratitude.

Two years flew by. During that time, I developed relationships with colleagues I'd never met in person but got to know over the phone. One day, the dedicated phone line we had for my interpreting services rang. This was unusual since my work shift had ended.

"Janet, I've got something to share with you." The familiar Cantonese accent told me I was speaking with the company's personnel manager.

I sat up straight. "I'm listening."

"We've been receiving letters from our clients about your interpreting performance."

My muscles immediately tightened. "What are they saying? Did I do something wrong?"

"Not at all. They're commending you for your high level of customer service and the prompt interpretation you render. We want you and your husband to fly to California and receive our Interpreter of the Year award."

It was a good thing I was seated. "Wow! Thank you."

What an honor. What a blessing. But even before I hung up, my mind was racing a different direction. If I met my employers in person, I'd have to confess I was blind. Gulp! How would they react?

Chapter Twenty
Timely Technology

Commit to the LORD whatever you do, and your plans will succeed.

—Proverbs 16:3

Our flight landed in Monterey, California. As Gene and I drove along the coastline, he described the breathtaking scenery of ocean waves crashing against rocks and white foam shooting into the air. But what took my breath away were the heights to which God had taken me. God's Word promises that *He is able to do immeasurably more than all we ask or imagine according to His power that is at work within us* (Ephesians 3:20).

This was so true in my own life. I could have never imagined I'd be performing my responsibilities well enough to attract the attention of upper management and receive an award from the largest over-the-phone interpreting company in the world. But the award I stored in my heart was far greater—the trophy of God's faithfulness.

Once in the hotel room, Gene and I got ready for the event. I slipped into a royal blue silk dress Gene had bought for me and put on my black high heels. I'd mastered the makeup applying task, but I took extra care this time. With my fingertips, I made sure my hair was just so. "Okay, I think I'm ready."

Gene placed his hand on my waist. "You look beautiful."

We crossed the luxurious hotel lobby toward a large banquet hall where the award dinner would be held. As we stepped inside, friendly voices greeted us. "You must be Janet. Is this your husband?"

I nodded. "Yes."

We were directed to our table. Once we settled into our seats, various people came by to introduce themselves. So far, no one had noticed my lack of vision. Being sighted for most of my life, I hadn't lost the natural tendency to look in the direction of the voice addressing me, so I displayed no mannerisms to reveal I couldn't see. And since none of us had met in person before, I wasn't expected to recognize anyone. Though I did recognize one voice from conversations with the corporate office.

"Kate, right?" I asked.

She hugged me. "So good to finally meet you, Janet."

I gripped her arm. "Can I confide in you, Kate? I know you're not aware, but I thought I should let you know that I'm blind."

"No way!" Kate pulled her arm away. Her exclamation echoed around the room. Then she leaned closer. "Blind? Totally? How much can you see?"

I directed a big smile toward her voice. "Yes, totally blind. I see nothing. Hard to tell over the phone, right?"

Kate let out a hearty laugh. "Yup, hard to tell over the phone."

I leaned toward her. "I'm not sure who needs to know. But I don't want to catch anyone by surprise."

"Don't you worry," she whispered in my ear. "Here's what we'll do. I will walk you up onto the stage. Once you receive your award, you can tell everybody then."

I winked at her. "Perfect. That's the plan."

After a scrumptious dinner, the president of the company addressed the large crowd, detailing the successes of the year. He praised the interpreters for our hard work. One by one, he presented various awards to several interpreters and staff.

He then paused dramatically. "And now for the top award of Interpreter of the Year. This year our award goes to an exemplary interpreter who displays constant professionalism, high performance, excellent customer service, and outstanding work ethic. With no further ado, the award of Interpreter of the Year goes to Janet Eckles."

Applause filled the room. Holding Kate's arm, I made my way from the table onto the stage. Once she'd helped me to the podium, Kate handed me a microphone. I cleared my throat, trying to keep calm.

"Thank you, everyone. I really don't deserve this award because it wasn't me who earned it but Christ Jesus in whom I've put my trust who made all this possible." I paused for a moment. "If you haven't noticed, I happen to be blind. If it wasn't for God's help, I most definitely wouldn't be here or able to do this job at all."

My tears flowed as more applause filled the room. After I stepped off the stage, colleagues and managers came by our table one by one to congratulate me. Many of them whispered as they hugged me, "Thank you for giving credit to God. I'm a Christian too, and I appreciate you being outspoken about your faith."

Gene and I got back to our hotel room too late to check on the boys. We'd never been away from them more than a day or two, but the activities the company had planned for us kept us in California longer. Once home, a surprise waited for me. Peggy, my dear blind friend who'd started out as my braille teacher, had left me a voice mail. "Call me. I've got something exciting to show you."

I returned her call, but her news didn't impress me. She had a new computer with a software that read aloud any words on the screen. I had zero experience with technology, much less in operating a computer, so nothing about that scenario attracted me. I thanked her for the information and hung up. But when I shared the details of her call with Gene, his reaction contradicted mine. "Let's at least go check it out."

I reluctantly agreed. We went to Peggy's home. She led me by the hand to her office. "I'll sit here and show you how it works."

When Peggy pressed a key, I heard the letter she'd chosen out loud. She typed a word, and I heard that too. She pressed other keys, and the computer read the entire sentence with such a clear, human-like voice as if a tiny person sat inside the computer.

"So cool!" I tapped her arm. "Can I try?"

She stood up, and I took her place in her office chair. "Tell me what to press."

"Just type a word."

Since I'd learned to type competently back in high school, my fingers immediately found the home keys. As I typed away, each letter I pressed echoed in the room. "Peggy, this is way too cool."

Peggy waited until I'd stopped typing. "Now hold down the control key and tap the left arrow key."

When I did, the computer read aloud the word I'd just typed. Wow!

"Amazing!" Gene's voice came from behind me. "What a great tool this could be for you."

I turned toward his voice. "Well, big boy, order one for me."

"Done," he said.

I paused for a moment and realized this was one more revelation of how God knows exactly what we need even before we speak it. Once my new computer equipped with a screen reader arrived, my first step was memorizing dozens of key commands. With the help of a trainer, I learned them quickly. Before long, using a combination of key strokes, I was able to write text, open emails, send them, create documents, edit, format them, and navigate the internet in the same way a sighted person does using the computer mouse.

But God's grace had no limits. One day I received a surprise phone call from my employer's training management team. "Your performance has been consistently excellent as you already know from the feedback you receive. We'd like to invite you to join our service observation team."

Me observe other interpreters' performance? My stomach had churned when I'd learned my calls were being monitored without my knowledge. But the positive feedback of my performance had humbled me with gratitude. Now I could pass on that useful experience to others. I took a deep breath. "I'm honored. Thank you. Of course, I'll do my best."

As time went on, some trainers must have forgotten I was blind. They assigned tasks of not only monitoring other interpreters' performance but also delivering training to new interpreters.

Days later, Gene placed two large books in my hands. "This came in the mail. It's for you from your company."

As I held them in my hands, I paused to pray. *Dear Lord, I really need You in this endeavor. I'm not sure how to manage this new challenge. Without being able to see and read these printed pages, it just seems impossible.*

God's answer came immediately. *Is there anything too difficult for God?* (Genesis 18:14).

I clung to that truth as I spent hours and hours scanning the training manual pages and converting them into Word documents. I then "read" them using my computer's screen reader. Choosing highlights, I created my own manual to deliver over-the-phone training to interpreters located across the U.S. and other countries.

In addition to interpreting, I served as a trainer for medical, finance, legal, insurance, and several other industries.

Since all was done over the phone, no one knew or even suspected that I'd delivered training sessions without sight. For me, this was one more proof that for God nothing is impossible.

Because of these new responsibilities my workdays became more demanding. Our sons' activities were also increasing as they grew older. In consequence, Gene and I began frequently missing our prayer time together.

One evening while our sons slept, Gene came downstairs to find me preparing their lunches for the next day in the kitchen. Pulling out a chair, he sat down at the kitchen table. "I got a call today from Monroe. Actually, from their president."

Something was clearly up. Zipping the sandwich bags closed, I frowned. "Who's that?"

"It's a company downtown, small but with great potential. They're struggling financially and want me to come on as their CFO to help them get going again."

I paused my lunch making. "Wait a minute. They're struggling so they want you to leave the great job you have and go work for them?"

Gene sighed. "I'd feel badly if I could help them but didn't."

His approach took me by surprise. So much so that I failed to ask God for guidance. Even worse, I reacted with my emotions. "Well, I think that's a terrible idea. How could you leave a perfectly good job for something you're not sure you can fix?"

We entered into a battle, and he won. Two weeks later, he resigned from his job and took the CFO position at the struggling company. Neither one of us expected the explosion that was about to happen.

CHAPTER TWENTY-ONE
NEVER TOO TIGHT TO TITHE

Honor the LORD with your wealth, with the first fruits of all your crops; then your barns will be filled to overflowing.

—Proverbs 3:9-10

Some weeks after taking on the CFO position at this company, Gene left me a voicemail. "I won't make it home for dinner tonight. I still have a long way to go with these financial reviews. Sorry, babe."

I huffed. That same message had been repeated way too many times each week. Gene believed he was saving this company, but soon our family time would be what needed rescuing. Even before his voice mail ended, I pressed the delete key with force.

After finishing my interpreting shift for the day, I sat with Jeff and Jason at the kitchen table. Jason pulled a paper out of his bookbag and placed it in my hands. "This is a note from my teacher."

I gave the wrinkled paper back to him. "Can you read it to Mommy, please?"

My sons never complained about reading communications from their school to me. As a bonus, their reading improved as they were forced to pronounce difficult words included in notes addressed to parents. I served the evening meal, leaving out Gene's place setting. They had headed upstairs to get ready for Bible stories and bedtime when Gene finally walked in from work. "Sorry again, babe! I tried to get away earlier but just couldn't."

I pulled out his dinner plate from the refrigerator and popped it into the microwave to warm. "You must know I'm not happy at all with this new arrangement. You're so stressed. Is all this worth it?"

Gene's only response was an uncomfortable silence. As days went on, I refrained from adding to his stress by complaining. Instead, I focused on the care of our sons. One evening during bedtime, I walked into Joe's room and encountered something unusual. The room was quiet, so I assumed he was already asleep. Stepping carefully toward his bed, I followed the side of the bed with my fingertips. Locating the pillow, I bent over to kiss my son. But instead of his chubby cheek, I encountered his toes. He'd burrowed under the covers headfirst.

"Hey you," I laughed. "What are you doing?"

He rustled out of the bedding. "Did I trick you?"

I found his cheek and pinched it lightly. "You sure did. Next time I'll be the one tricking you, young man."

I relished when my sons took my blindness as a natural part of our family rather than an obstacle that could cause sadness or worry. One afternoon as Jeff dashed out the patio doors, he stopped. "Mommy, is Daddy coming home to take me to soccer practice?"

I wanted to respond with the truth. "No, honey, your father is working late tonight again. Obviously, helping a struggling business is more important than his family."

But I swallowed those words and said instead, "Nope, sweet boy. Tommy's mom will be here soon to take you."

Month after month, our routine didn't change. I memorized Bible verses, recited them out loud, and my sons repeated them. Little by little, they ended up memorizing the verses as well. As they grew, the Bible passages we memorized became longer and more complex. One evening, the four of us climbed onto our king-sized bed. "Hey guys, no more jumping. Everyone, sit down."

Wrapping my arm around my youngest son, Joe, I went on, "Now all of you pay attention. Who can tell me about the armor of God? What different parts does it include?"

Jason surged upright. "Me, me! I want to go first."

"Go ahead. Jeff and Joe, listen and see if he misses anything."

Jason began. "The helmet of salvation. The breastplate of righteousness. The shield of faith. The belt of truth. The sword of the Word of God. The shoes to spread peace."

"Nope," Jeff chimed in. "It's the shoes of peace to spread the gospel."

"Jeff is right." I ran my fingers through Jason's curly, black hair. "Good job, though. But next time say it slower so you think about what God is saying to us."

One Sunday morning as we drove to Mass, I turned to Gene. "How much longer will these long hours at the office last?"

I tried to sound understanding, but my words didn't reflect the resentment rumbling inside of me. Gene sighed. "I'm doing my best. We need more contracts, more revenue. But there's a bigger issue."

To my perspective, there was certainly a bigger issue. Gene had left his other job with a good salary and normal office hours so he could have time for his family. Now business problems consumed his time and attention.

I tried to keep sarcasm out of my voice. "So, what would this bigger issue be?"

"Well, I reviewed all the company records going back a year or so. The company is not only in the red but owes FICA taxes to the IRS."

"Wow, they're in big trouble," I commented. "You don't fool around with the IRS."

Two months later, we learned just how devastating this "bigger issue" really was. The company president and vice-president made the decision to file bankruptcy and close the doors. I didn't know if I should cheer and be relieved or lament that Gene no longer had a job.

Fortunately, finding new positions had always been easy for Gene. But far more devastating was news we received in the mail. The letter's complicated legalese notified us the 100% Penalty Law applied to us. I gasped. "Penalty? What in the world does that mean? How does it apply to us?"

Gene inhaled deeply. "According to that law, when a business owes FICA taxes to the IRS and the company folds, the officers are personally responsible for the debt."

"That means the president and vice-president, right?"

"It also means me as the CFO. But don't worry. We'll figure it out."

"We?" I gritted my teeth. "What do you mean, 'we'? You were only with them for six months. Why should we owe a penny?"

Gene took my hand. "Calm down, honey. Don't worry. It's all good."

Furiously, I pulled my hand from his. "No, it's not all good. Just how much do *we* owe?"

"Two hundred and fifty thousand dollars."

My body went numb. "How much? So why don't the two company owners pay it? Why us?"

Gene let out a deep sigh. "Well, I didn't tell you this, but they both filed personal bankruptcy. The IRS won't come against them."

I struggled to speak. "So, you're saying we have to pay the entire two hundred and fifty thousand!"

Slumping down onto the couch, I pressed my face in my hands. I was too angry to cry, too horrified to speak. Gene sat down beside me. "Somehow, we'll do it."

That night I cried out to God. *Lord, how could this happen to us? Give us some solutions! This is so horribly unfair!*

Every moment I could, I slipped on my earphones and listened to God's Word. Peace came when I pondered on verses like Proverbs 3:5 that reminded me to trust in the Lord with all my heart and not lean on my own understanding.

But Gene and I now faced a huge monster, and we needed our combined strength to defeat it. Each time we received demands from the IRS, we prayed together, asking for strength and solutions. When we found no solutions, we prayed for wisdom. Gene did find one of the few attorneys that dealt with the 100% Penalty Law.

After their initial conversation, Gene hung up the phone. "I can't believe it. Twenty thousand dollars is the attorney's retainer fee to represent us."

In a matter of weeks, the IRS had taken possession of all our savings, including the college funds we'd set up for our boys. They determined what were necessary expenses—mortgage, food, and utilities. Any other expenses such as Catholic school tuition were considered unnecessary, so those funds belonged to the IRS. The most difficult time of the day for me was when the mail arrived. Gene would rip open an envelope. "Another letter from the IRS."

As he read the content, my muscles tightened and my heart raced. Some letters informed us of a judge's ruling against us, summoned us for another hearing, or notified us of the new IRS agent assigned to us. They often demanded more financial records to prove they had seized all they could from us.

Gene and I borrowed from my parents and friends, took out a line of credit, and did all we could to gather funds for legal fees and attorney's bills. Several times a day, we held hands and pleaded with God for guidance, mercy, and His intervention. Our prayer time always calmed our hearts and gave us enough determination to face each day. But the full penalty levied against us remained unchanged, and as the process continued, all the court rulings were against us.

Lying awake one night with tears of anger still flowing, I made a commitment to God. *Lord, if You will show us the way out, I vow to make this frightening episode a testimony of Your faithfulness.*

Throughout this ordeal, our family had never missed Sunday Mass. And no matter how low our bank account got, Gene and I were still committed to giving our tithes each week. A few weeks later, another corporate headhunter contacted Gene. After a series of interviews, he accepted a position. The retail company he'd be working for was an hour commute from home, but at this point the distance didn't matter. We both praised God for this job offer and income to begin paying what we borrowed.

Eventually, our attorney announced that he'd reached a settlement with the IRS. We were relieved until we learned that the amount was greater than what we had. As I lay awake at night beside Gene, everything in me wanted to lash out and blame him for getting us into this nightmare. But God's whisper to trust in Him still echoed in me.

I turned toward Gene. "Only a miracle from God will get us out of this."

The next evening, Gene walked in the door after work. "I had a thought coming home. Maybe it sounds crazy, but I'm going to ask for an advance in my salary."

I stared in his direction. "I've never heard of anyone doing that. Especially when they've just started the job. They will definitely think you're crazy."

"All I can do is try."

I said nothing further but silently prayed to God for this possibility that in truth did seem impossible. But much to our amazement, when Gene went ahead and asked, his new employer agreed. That advance amount plus an additional bank loan sufficed to cover our settlement with the IRS. When we received official confirmation that our case had been closed, I dropped to my knees in thanksgiving to God for setting us free from that IRS prison. Though we still faced loans everywhere, our hearts burst with gratitude to God for sustaining us through months of agonizing turmoil.

What we didn't expect was that a new test would soon be upon us.

Chapter Twenty-Two
The Sunshine of God's Love

So do not fear, for I am with you; do not be dismayed, for I am your God. I will strengthen you and help you; I will uphold you with my righteous right hand.

—Isaiah 41:10

One evening, Gene came home, plopped on the couch, and let out a long breath. "One year, that's all it lasted."

I put down the towel I was folding. "What are you talking about?"

His silence told me all I needed to know. Recent local news had reported the financial failing of Gene's employer, one of the largest retail discount stores. Several financial publications had predicted the company would fold. And now it had.

Lord, You gave him this job! I cried out silently. *And now it's gone. Your ways of giving and taking away leave me baffled.*

Typically, I never argued with God no matter what the circumstances. But this time I did. Over and over again, I asked how God could take something He Himself had given us? Trying to control my tears, I ran for shelter to God's Word.

> "For my thoughts are not your thoughts, neither are your ways my ways," declared the Lord.
>
> —Isaiah 55:8

Despite the confusion in my heart, peace returned as I forced myself to truly believe that God's Word is still trustworthy and His promises true. Life went on. Without Gene's income, our hope of paying our loans faded as did our expectation for a life free from debt.

At night in bed, we held hands and prayed. Gene reminded me how God had led us in the past from valleys to mountaintops, from lack of funds to answers. After a few moments in silence, we vowed to face this new challenge differently. We would continue our constant prayer. But no matter what happened, we would also thank God. Even when we saw no possibilities on the horizon, we committed to praising God again and again for the doors He would open.

By this point, Gene had gone through enough job searches that corporate headhunters in his field all knew him. It wasn't long before he'd been offered another interview. But this time the position would require a major change for us. Hanging up the phone with the headhunter, Gene turned to me. "Hey, baby, what would you think about moving to Florida?"

"In a second," I grinned, assuming he was joking.

"Well, Disney World has a position for manager of merchandise. If we're interested, I will need to fly to New York for an interview."

"Are you serious?" I gasped. "Let's ask the boys and see what they say."

All three jumped at the possibility. "Yeah, Dad, let's go. How cool is that?"

Then Gene got another phone call from the headhunter. "No need to come to New York. Turns out the vice-president at Disney World already knows you. He wants you to fly directly to Orlando."

Gene booked his flight. After his interview, he called home. "I've got some bad news. They didn't offer me the manager position."

"That's okay," I interrupted. "It just wasn't meant to be. God has something else for you."

"He sure does!" Gene chuckled. "After reviewing my experience and work history, I guess they changed their minds about what position I'd best fit here."

I sat up straight. "To what?"

"Well, they felt I was overqualified for the manager position. So, they offered me the position of director of merchandise instead."

I fell silent, pondering. So that's what God meant when He said His ways are above ours (Isaiah 55:8). He'd had all this planned from the beginning. When we chose to praise God instead of lamenting and whining, His mighty hand had moved on our behalf.

Before putting our St. Louis house on the market and moving to Orlando, decisions needed to be made. For one, leaving my parents behind now that my father had also lost his sight would be painful for all of us. By this time, Abuelita had passed away. My brother Ed was married and lived with his wife in Wisconsin. We saw them several times a year, and now that we were adults, my brother and I had put aside our childhood conflicts and were very close.

As we pondered what to do about my parents, Gene had a solution. "I think your mom and dad should come with us. We'll just have to find a house big enough."

I called my parents and gave them the invitation. Mom sighed with contentment. "No more cold winters and live in Florida instead? It's a dream come true!"

Disney's relocating department assigned us a real estate agent. When we arrived in Orlando, the agent met with us. "I have a perfect neighborhood in mind in a lovely area between the airport and Disney World."

The warm weather in January reminded us that we were indeed in the sunshine state. Holding hands, Gene and I took time for prayer before we began the house hunting process. "Lord, lead us to the house You have chosen for us."

As we visited dozens of houses, my mind was frazzled trying to remember each layout. The agent reviewed a new listing on her phone. "This one just popped up. One of its features is an in-law quarters."

When we walked through the property, I knew immediately this was the house God had for us. I gave silent thanks. *It's perfect, Lord, large enough for three generations to live under one roof comfortably!*

Our offer was accepted, and we signed the contract. But as I sat in the airplane to fly back to St. Louis and pack, hesitation attacked me. I'd navigated through our St. Louis home with no problem. How long would it take me before I could navigate comfortably in an unfamiliar house?

Our friends in St. Louis knew about my blindness and accepted it. How would new acquaintances in Orlando react?

Lord, help me make this work! I prayed fervently. *Please guide me in this new, strange place.*

Packing up, we moved our sons, parents, furniture, and other belongings to Orlando. We also brought with us the burden of many loans that weighed heavily on our hearts. Though the IRS ordeal was behind us, we still owed my parents and friends as well as the bank.

But as we embraced the promises of God's Word, confidence drove out doubt. God had already performed miracles for us beyond what we'd ever imagined. We didn't need to know how He would do it again. We just needed to have faith that He would.

And indeed, God did bless once again beyond what we could have imagined. In addition to Gene's new salary, which was not only double what he'd expected and included attractive benefits, it also offered stock options. And Gene exercised all of these.

It wasn't long before he called me from his office at Disney World. "We have enough now to pay all our loans to everyone we owe."

Once our debts were paid off, our savings began growing like never before. We'd not only witnessed God's promises to prevail, but He'd taught us what it meant to trust Him with every unexpected test that entered our lives.

But the next ordeal wasn't just a test. This time, it was a huge exam.

CHAPTER TWENTY-THREE
MYSTERY SOLVED

If I rise on the wings of the dawn, if I settle on the far side of the sea, even there your hand will guide me, your right hand will hold me fast.

—Psalm 139:9-10

I held the phone between my shoulder and chin while I unpacked box after box of items the movers had left piled up all over our new Orlando house. As I put clothes away, I called churches and local high schools. "Can you tell me if you have any Christian organizations for teenagers?"

I got numerous leads and names. By the time I'd moved all the empty boxes into the garage, Jeff and Joe were signed up for Student Venture, a Christian ministry in the high school they'd both be attending. Jason had graduated from his Catholic high school in St. Louis just before our move. A year after arriving in

Orlando, he began a program in computer animation at a prestigious Florida college. Months later, he rented his own apartment, so we saw far less of him than we wished.

My next task once we were completely unpacked was to learn to navigate my new home. I counted steps and memorized the location of each piece of furniture, distance between each piece, location of the staircase, and any other details to give me a point of reference. Soon I was able to walk around the house with ease.

My parents had settled happily into their new in-law quarters as well, though they spent much of their time with the rest of us in the main part of the house. Having three generations living under one roof worked well. Mom and I developed a routine where she prepared dinner and I took care of laundry, cleaning, and lunches for the boys. There was nothing Mom wouldn't offer to help with, and her joyful personality filled our home with a sweetness uniquely hers.

She also became my best cheerleader, always praising me for the tasks I managed. Even more so when I received certificates of commendations from my employer. Sometimes I came home from work conferences with trophies recognizing my performance. Mom put together a portfolio showcasing my accomplishments, which she insisted on showing to anyone willing to sit and listen.

Meanwhile, my father spent his days listening to audiobooks or working outdoors in the fruit orchard he was developing behind the swimming pool. White cane in hand, he even managed to dig a trench on his own, creating an irrigation system to water his fruit trees.

My parents also handled the grocery shopping. Once a week, Mom guided my father to the garage, where Mom got behind the wheel of their car. Together, they drove to the grocery store, where they slowly ambled through the aisles and made their choices. Once home, they divided the grocery items, some to their fridge and cupboards, others to ours. Always neat and orderly, Mom kept every detail of food storage organized, which made meal preparations easier.

But our family move to Orlando revealed that not everything in Mom's life was as orderly as we'd all thought. In fact, we were stunned at what we learned. One day she called me into the living room. She'd been going through the last of the boxes she and my father had brought with them from St. Louis. She lifted up a sheaf of papers. When I touched it, my fingers told me the papers were old and well-worn.

"These are all the records we brought from Bolivia." she said. I could hear puzzled confusion in her tone. "The one on top is my birth certificate from Peru, where I was born before your grandfather moved our family to Bolivia. For some reason, my birth date given there is different than the one in my baptismal record."

This didn't seem a big deal to me. After all, mistakes in bureaucratic recordkeeping were common enough in Bolivia. But the error along with the fact that Mom had been an only child brought to mind my aunt Laura's wild, angry accusations in my childhood that Mom wasn't truly a member of her family. I hadn't been back to La Paz since we'd left more than thirty years earlier when I was just twelve years old. As the mystery of Mom's conflicting records stirred curiosity in me, I felt a sudden yearning to visit my old home.

"I think it's time I go back and visit the family in La Paz," I commented thoughtfully.

Mom took my hand. "No, I don't want you traveling by yourself. It's not safe."

I kissed her cheek. "Now don't you be worrying about me. I'll take my white cane and get an escort."

I made the flight arrangements. When I landed in La Paz, one of my cousins picked me up from the airport. Over the next few days, I had a wonderful time visiting with relatives, catching up on all the family news, and filling them in on what my own family was doing in the United States. I was also able to reconnect with the daughter of my mom's cousin Laura, whom I'd babysat as an infant.

After some mutual reminiscing, I asked, "Do you think your mother might know anything about my mom possibly being adopted?"

"She might," my cousin admitted cautiously.

She and I visited Laura, who lived alone. Almost seventy years old, Laura appeared to have overcome her mental illness and seemed to be in good health. I explained why I had come.

"When I was a child, you mentioned that Mom wasn't a member of your family biologically. Does that mean she was adopted? I would greatly appreciate any information you could give me about Mom being adopted or whatever you might know about her story."

Laura was silent for a moment. Then she said slowly, "I don't actually know much. But I know someone who does."

She gave me the name and number of an old woman who lived in a small town near Lima, Peru. I called the number and explained who I was. "My mom's cousin Laura gave me this number and told me you might know something about a baby named Lucy being adopted almost seventy years ago." I gave her the family name of my grandfather. "They moved to Bolivia when my mom was still an infant. Her married name is Perez."

There was silence on the phone line. Then the woman said, "Yes, I remember that baby. I was there when a couple took her away."

The woman gave additional details. That couple was Abuelita and my grandfather who had been married for several years at this time, and they still had no children. They'd traveled to this small Peruvian town in search of a treatment for Abuelita's infertility. The local doctor, whose name was Benavente, was famous for his expertise in using non-traditional indigenous and East Asian medical practices to heal people, including for infertility.

He was equally popular for his handsome appearance and charm, which he used to capture the hearts of women wherever he visited. In consequence, he'd fathered at least twenty children the family knew about with multiple mothers.

Dr. Benavente examined Abuelita, heard her story, and gave the bad news. She could not have children.

Abuelita broke down in sobs. This seemed to touch Dr. Benavente's heart. As my grandfather tried to console her, Dr. Benavente stepped out of his office. Crossing the courtyard, he entered the house.

Inside was a local woman who was cradling a two-month-old baby girl in her arms. Playing beside her were two-year-old twin boys. The woman I was talking with on the phone, a Benavente family member, was there as well. Walking in, Dr. Benavente reached out to take the baby. When the woman resisted, he forced the baby from her arms. Carrying the two-month-old child back to his office, he thrust the baby toward Abuelita, "Here! This is your baby."

Like Abuelita, Dr. Benavente was of European blood with hazel eyes, and by appearance, the baby could easily have been Abuelita's birth child. Elated and grateful, Abuelita and Grandfather left his office with that baby girl. There were no adoption papers or other documents, only Dr. Benavente's choice to give his own daughter to Abuelita and Grandfather. As it was simple back then, Abuelita and Grandfather returned to Bolivia and planned to register baby Lucy as having been born to Abuelita.

The woman on the phone concluded. "But that's all I know."

I tried to record each detail in my head. "What about the woman who was the baby's birth mother? Or the twin boys? Do you know anything about where they ended up?"

"I don't know anything about the mother. But the twins now live in Lima and are both veterinarians."

That piece of information helped. Researching in phone directories, Laura's daughter and I found a phone number for a Dr. Benavente. Once I arrived back in Orlando, I sat Mom down. "I have some interesting news."

When she heard the details, Mom gasped. "I can't believe it. So, Laura was right. All this time, I wasn't biologically part of her family. We all thought she was crazy. Especially since Abuelita always insisted she was lying. Do you think this Dr. Benavente in Lima belongs to my birth family?"

"If we call this number, we can ask," I assured her.

"No, no!" Mom's voice was shaky. "If this isn't real, they'll think we're crazy."

"We'll have to take that chance." Picking up the phone, I dialed the number. A man's voice answered. I took a deep breath, then asked anxiously, "Is this Dr. Benavente who has a veterinarian practice in Lima?"

"Yes, it is. How can I help you?"

In a rush of words, I explained why I was calling. "My name is Janet. My mother's name is Lucy Perez Arenas. We've recently learned she was adopted many years ago in Peru and that her birth father's name was Dr. Benavente." I gave the name of the town where Dr. Benavente had practiced medicine. "We wondered if perhaps you might be related."

There was complete silence. I thought at first the man I'd called must have hung up. I spoke again. "Hello?"

Finally, I heard a stuttering male voice. "What…what did you say?"

I repeated my explanation. When I finished, the man spoke again, this time with deep emotion choking his voice. "Yes, Lucy is the sister we've always heard about. Our mother told us she was given away to a couple who took her to Bolivia. No one in the family ever knew what became of her."

"Well, she's right here," I said, trying to contain my excitement. "Would you like to speak to her?"

"Oh, yes, please."

I handed the phone to Mom. She shed tears as she conversed with her new-found sibling. At sixty-seven years of age, her life had changed. She was no longer an only child but had at least twenty siblings. The woman who cared for her during her first two months wasn't her biological mother and most of the other siblings had different mothers. All but six had passed away by this time.

After the phone conversation, Mom and I reviewed everything we'd learned. She gasped with each new detail. Suddenly, she paused, then said thoughtfully. "Wait a minute. I remember Abuelita kept a picture of twin boys in the drawer of her nightstand. When she showed me that picture, she told me the boys were sons of a well-respected doctor in Peru."

I quickly made arrangements for Mom and my father to travel to Lima and meet her new family. Mom discovered that she and her older twin brothers shared the same stature, mannerisms, passionate joy, and quick expressions of affection.

During the years while Mom was growing up in Bolivia, the Benavente brothers had also risen to an elite level in Lima's society. Now they embraced their little sister as a new-found gem that brought a beautiful sparkle to the last years of their lives.

CHAPTER TWENTY-FOUR
SAYING GOODBYE TO RELIGION

As the deer pants for streams of water, so my soul pants for you,
O God. My soul thirsts for God, for the living God.

—Psalm 42:1-2

As the months swept by, we all continued to blossom in the sunshine state. Jason was doing well in college. Jeff and Joe continued to participate in Christian youth activities through Student Venture ministries and were also attending a youth Bible study. They both excelled in every sport they tried. In fact, Joe eventually became captain of his football team and the lacrosse team as well. Joe and Jeff also played on All-Star teams for our county.

But though we'd all settled well into our new life in Orlando, Sunday church attendance had become a battleground. Looping my purse over my shoulder one Sunday morning, I called, "C'mon, guys, get downstairs. We're leaving for church."

"Mom, I'm already going to Student Venture meetings," Joe called back from the top of the stairs. "Not to mention Bible study every week So why do I have to go to Mass? I don't get anything out of it."

I rolled my eyes. "Fine. Stay home."

Joe had a way about him that always managed to convince me. And though I wouldn't admit to him or Gene that his logic made sense, I secretly agreed with Joe. I found no spiritual food for my soul in attending Mass nor any spiritual growth in repeating memorized prayers. Most disappointing was Holy Communion, which had lost all meaning in the ritualistic way it was presented. I left church each Sunday hungry for more of God's Word and thirsty for a closer relationship with my Savior.

One afternoon, Gene and I sat at the patio table on our pool deck. A warm breeze lifted my hair as I commented thoughtfully, "What I really want is to find a church Bible study like the one I visited in St. Louis when I first lost my sight. Remember?"

Gene cleared his throat as he always did when something made him uncomfortable. I guessed mention of that painful season in our marriage was stirring memories of his infidelity. "I remember. In fact, I rather expected you'd keep attending there."

"I should have," I sighed. "But maybe I can find a Bible study around here."

Research eventually led me to a local Baptist church that offered a women's Bible study. I didn't care about the denomination. All I wanted was to satisfy my hunger for more of Jesus and more of God's Word. I wanted to learn what certain Bible passages meant when I listened to them and what God was offering in His promises.

Each of those desires became reality as I began spending week after week with those precious Baptist ladies studying God's Word. One evening when Gene picked me up after Bible study, I asked, "What would you think about attending one of their Sunday services?"

"What?" he responded with astonishment. "But we're Catholic, and that's a Baptist church."

Enjoying life in Florida.

"And your point? They follow the Bible, and that's what we need. That's what our sons need too."

After a long silence, Gene mumbled. "Okay, I'll go with you but only once."

I understood his hesitation since I too was fighting the ingrained doctrine we'd been taught that the Catholic Church was the only real church. I tried to ignore memories of my father's younger brother, now a prominent Catholic archbishop in Bolivia, who had reminded me over and over again, "You're Catholic. Never forget that."

The following Sunday was sunny, and birds sang as we got into the car. My heart also sang because we were about to step into a new, but meaningful, spiritual terrain. I held Gene's hand for guidance as we drew close to the entrance of the Baptist church. We were smiling like two teenagers self-consciously aware they were breaking school rules. Were we betraying our religion by attending this church?

Months and months of studying God's Word gave me the answer. The Bible said I was God's child and co-heir with Jesus. My devotion was to God, and my allegiance was to God's Word, not to a religion.

Gene and I sat in a back pew. Leaning close to my ear, Gene quietly described the décor, which was simple but reverent. No fancy vestments for the pastor. No elaborate altar. We found the simplicity refreshing, and the pastor's preaching immediately captivated us. The reading of Bible passages, explanations of biblical teaching, illustrations, and life application were all delightfully new to us and oh so different from the rote liturgy of Mass.

From our first visit, South Orlando Baptist became our home church, and we never again went back to the Catholic Church. A new world had opened up for me. With each Sunday sermon and Bible study, the verses that had been engraved on my heart from listening to them on cassette became increasingly and beautifully clear in their meaning and application to my life.

My parents were far less happy about our change in church attendance. Father approached me angrily. "What do you think you're doing? You're Catholic. You don't belong in those Protestant churches."

Mom's reaction was more composed. "Honey, you go where they teach the Bible. I would go with you, but I can't. I have to go with your father."

To our delight, Joe and Jeff no longer argued about attending church with us. Though they weren't always enthusiastic about participating in Christian activities, they enjoyed the youth program at South Orlando Baptist and seemed to grow spiritually there. Although we invited Jason to join us, he resisted. Since he attended a Catholic church and school all his life, he felt no need to change.

One day Joe walked in the front door from football practice and tossed his gym bag on the floor. "Where's my favorite mom?"

"In the kitchen, my football star."

Before I knew it, he picked me up as if I were a child and twirled me in the air. I tried to keep from laughing. "Put me down. Put me down right now."

Setting me down, Joe kissed my cheek. "I love you, Mom."

"I love you too, you stinker." I gave him a teasing frown. "By the way, before you head upstairs, Coach Jones called about a Christian camp in North Carolina. It's run by the Fellowship of Christian Athletes. They even have professional athletes participating. And I would like you and Jeff to go."

Joe's tone took on a tinge of annoyance. "Mom, do we have to?"

"If you want to keep playing football, you're going," I said firmly. "Now hurry up and shower. It's almost dinner time."

Joe, captain of the football team.

While I set the table, Mom sat on the couch, reviewing her grocery list. As young boys, Joe and his older brothers couldn't pronounce Abuelita, or grandmother in Spanish. They came up with Ita, which became my mom's nickname to all who knew and loved her. Heading upstairs, Joe paused to give his grandmother a kiss. "Nice curlers, Ita. You'll be looking pretty. I might just take you out on a date."

Ita giggled. "Oh, you're my sweet boy."

Walking into the laundry room, I began emptying the dryer. Mom followed to offer her help. Using my usual staple system to sort the clothing, I told her, "Jeff and Joe are leaving for the weekend. It's a camp for Christian athletes. So, I need to make sure they have enough clean clothes."

"Here, then." Mom removed a pile of socks from my hands. "Let me pair these for you."

That weekend, Gene and I took Jeff and Joe to the FCA bus, which was packed full of noisy teenage boys. Among the many fun sports activities, the professional athletes participating in the camp shared their own testimonies of salvation with the teen campers. When Joe and Jeff returned from camp, Joe knocked on our bedroom door. "Mom, Dad, can we pray?"

My heart leapt at his request. "Sure."

Grasping our hands in his, Joe prayed aloud, "Lord, thank you for giving Your life for my sins and becoming my Savior. Thank you for giving me parents who pray with me."

He'd left me so speechless it took me some time to get the words out. "Joe, did you accept Jesus as your Savior this weekend at camp?"

"Sure did." With that, he walked out of the room.

I'd prayed for many years that God would touch my boys' hearts and draw them to Himself. But I was still beyond amazed at how beautifully God answered. I silently praised God over and over again.

When I spoke to Joe's coach later, he told me the details of what had happened that weekend at the FCA camp. "When the speaker asked if anyone was ready to give their life to God, Joe stood up. You know what a leader he is. Whatever he does, other boys follow. So, when he came forward, his friends followed and also accepted Christ as their Savior."

That wasn't the end. Defying our family rule against tattoos, Joe had a large cross tattooed on his left arm. When we complained, he told us, "If anyone asks me about it, I'll tell them about Jesus."

As always, his logic convinced us. Meanwhile, I continued to stay busy interpreting over the phone. But I also never stopped looking for new possibilities. One day, I had an audacious idea. Being a court-certified interpreter would open more doors for me. Maybe that would be asking for the impossible—or maybe not. It couldn't hurt to try.

"So sorry, ma'am," the secretary at the Orange County courthouse informed me when I called. "We don't have the test in braille, and we've never given it to the blind."

Never? With God, there is no such thing as never. Nor is there an obstacle He can't overcome or barrier He can't remove. I cleared my throat to muster up boldness. "That it hasn't been done before doesn't mean it can't be done. If you'll assign someone to read the written portions to me, I'll do the rest."

The courthouse clerk reluctantly agreed. For months, I spent day and night memorizing legal terminology. I also reviewed just about any court scenario imaginable. I studied until my brain sizzled. When the time finally came to take the test, I told my women's Bible study group, "I really need your prayers. I'll be taking a test and need God's help."

They agreed to pray for me, and I knew I could count on them to carry out their promise. When the test began, I used methods I'd developed to retain the multiple choices read to me so I could choose the correct answer. All through the test, I prayed silently for God's help and clarity of mind. A week later, the courthouse sent a letter informing me I'd passed all four parts of the test on my first try. That's how I became the first blind court-certified interpreter in Florida.

But another first was coming into my life. Not a happy first or one I ever dreamed I'd experience. But it was also a first that led to God becoming even more real to me.

Chapter Twenty-Five
He Became My Strength

Blessed are those who mourn, for they will be comforted.

—Matthew 5:4

All three of our sons were now out of high school, which gave me more free time for my own activities. When not occupied elsewhere, I spent my evenings at the computer. But this time, I focused on a personal project. I'd decided to write my story. One day my grandchildren would read about their blind grandmother who was guided by the white cane of faith in Christ Jesus.

Evening after evening, I wrote chapter after chapter. Months later, right before I reached the end of my story, I had an unanticipated and heartbreaking interruption. At nineteen, our youngest son Joe had landed a good job. He'd also started his first semester of college.

One Friday evening, Joe had gone out with his friends. Late that night, our middle son Jeff walked into our bedroom. "Joe's been hurt."

"What?" Horrified, I jumped out of bed. "What happened?"

"I don't know. They're taking him to the emergency room."

Throwing on our clothes, Gene and I rushed out the door and headed to the hospital. As we drove, we prayed frantically for Joe to be okay. We still had no idea what had happened or how seriously our son was hurt. Once we reached the hospital emergency room, we waited and waited for someone to let us know what was happening, praying continuously for Joe as we sat there.

Finally, a doctor walked up to us. "Are you the parents of Joe Eckles?"

Standing up, I took a step toward the doctor's voice. "Yes, we are. Where is he? What happened? When can we take him home?"

Holding me tightly, Gene broke in. "We haven't heard anything. We need some kind of update."

The doctor's voice turned immediately somber. "I'm so sorry. We did all we could. But the multiple stab wounds caused him to lose too much blood. He didn't make it. I'm so sorry for your loss."

Stab wounds? Loss? My body went numb. I couldn't breathe. Pressing my face into my hands, I slid into a tunnel of disbelief, battling to digest what the doctor just said. *Not my Joe, Lord! Not my baby!*

Closing my eyes, I tried to wake up from this nightmare. But I couldn't. This was real. Then in the midst of my agonizing pain, my heart heard clearly a loving voice that spoke with deep compassion. *Be still, Janet, and know that I am God* (Psalm 46:10).

A nurse pressed a pill into the palm of my hand. "Ma'am, take this please. Here's some water."

I pushed her hand away gently. "No, no thank you."

She probably expected I'd burst into hysterical wailing. But I didn't. Once again that verse echoed in my heart. "Be still and know that I am God." God was still the same God who had sustained me through so much. The same God who had lifted me when I was broken. The same God who had whispered His comfort when my world fell apart.

I pressed my fist against my forehead. *Lord, I know You're with me. Please don't leave me now! I need your strength.* Turning to my mom, who had joined us at the hospital, I held her tight as she sobbed uncontrollably.

The conversation between Gene and the doctors became a blur. We eventually drove home in an emotional fog. My body trembled, and my tears flowed. In the silence of night, I had an intimate conversation with God.

Yes, Lord, You are God, powerful and mighty. But how could You let this happen to us? We know you. We serve you. Joe knew you too. Why didn't you protect him? Your Word says that all things turn to good for those who love You and are called according to Your purpose. But I don't see how this horror of losing my son could ever turn to good. I want my Joe back. I want just one more chance to hug him and tell him I love him.

As the days went by, we learned more about the senseless events that had ended in the death of our son. He'd been with another friend when they'd stopped at a convenience store to make some purchases. There they'd seen another young man who had also stopped in at the convenience store with his girlfriend, a young

177

woman Joe had shown interest in several months before, though by this time Joe had another girlfriend.

Seeing Joe and his friend, the young man flew into a rage, pulled out a knife, and began stabbing them. The friend survived, but Joe did not. The man had been arrested on first-degree murder charges. The more we learned, the more questions poured from my heart.

Lord, I know my requests are not logical, but I can't make sense of this tragedy. I've tasted Your loving comfort, and I don't doubt Your promises will prevail. But how do I live with this pain that weighs a ton? How do I move forward without one of my sons whom You Yourself gave me? How long will it take for me to be free from this grief and overwhelming heartache?

Finally in one quiet moment, my ranting stopped, and I heard in my heart another sweet promise from God:

Then will the eyes of the blind be opened and the ears of the deaf unstopped. Then will the lame leap like a deer. (Isaiah 35:5-6)

Brushing away one last tear, I reflected on that promise. One day in heaven, I would see Joe again. And this time with my own eyes because in heaven there is no blindness. Exquisite hope filtered through my soul and eased my heartache as I grasped the wonderful truth that my separation from my youngest son was only temporary. I would indeed see him and hug him again. I would hear him say, "There's my favorite mom."

Days later, Gene and I sat across the desk of the funeral director. He placed a book before us. "Look through these pages and choose the coffin you want for Joe."

A chill went through me. I'd expected to choose Joe's graduation gift or the tuxedo for his wedding day. Instead, we had to choose his coffin. *Lord, this is a cruel thing to ask of any mother!* I cried out in my heart. *Hold on to me! I can't do it alone.*

Gene squeezed my hand. "Are you okay?"

I breathed in deeply. "Let's do this."

We worked out the details of Joe's memorial service for the morning of September 11, 2002. Gene and I would both speak. We'd requested a lit candle to be placed on top of Joe's coffin. The church overflowed with friends, family from St. Louis, and hundreds of high school students. Gene walked me to the pulpit. Standing before the microphone, I spoke with supernatural composure.

"Joe was a leader, skilled in many ways, talented in sports. Many of you knew him well. Many of you shared the same Bible study with Student Venture. Some of you received Christ as your Savior at the FCA camp along with Joe. But many of the rest of you may not have taken that step yet. Joe didn't know last Friday would be his last day on earth. Since Joe took steps to ensure his entrance into heaven, we know where he is today, in the mansion Jesus prepared for him. Who knows. Maybe he's throwing a football with other heavenly players right now. But more than setting an example of an excellent athlete, Joe's life was about serving a purpose."

I pointed in the direction of the coffin with its lit candle on top. "See that light? That light is a reminder that Joe is calling you, too, to accept Christ as your Savior. Despite being cut short, Joe's life wasn't in vain. God is using his death to remind us all that tomorrow is not guaranteed to any of us. Right now, in this moment, God is giving each of us the opportunity to choose where we'll spend eternity."

After the memorial service, the pastor hugged me. "I'm so sorry about Joe, Janet. But I just want to say that in twenty-five years of ministry, I've never seen a mother share the gospel at her child's memorial service. Thank you for doing that."

Reflecting on his comment, I realized God has also given my own pain a purpose. And that purpose was about to turn into something even more powerful.

CHAPTER TWENTY-SIX
OUT OF MY COMFORT ZONE

Trust in the LORD with all your heart and lean not on your own understanding; in all your ways acknowledge him, and he will make your paths straight.

—Proverbs 3:5-6

Gene's sobbing woke me up in the middle of the night. Turning toward him, I placed my hand on his arm. "Do you think we should go to grief counseling?"

He got out of bed. "I . . . don't know. I'm okay."

Of course, he wasn't okay. Nor was I. Three weeks had passed since we said goodbye to our Joe, and the pain still seared. The next day, I called our church. The secretary listed a few options. "Here's a group that offers support for parents who have lost a child, but it's not Christian based."

Gene and I decided we needed to learn how other parents dealt with this trauma. Arriving at the community building where the group was scheduled to meet, Gene and I walked down the long corridors to the meeting place. A hush covered the room, and I sensed heavy gloom. As we took our seats and waited for the meeting to begin, I could hear sniffles coming from various directions around me. One woman seated directly in front of us was sobbing inconsolably.

Leaning forward, I tapped her shoulder. "Are you okay?"

"No! How can a mother who lost her son be okay? I lost him a year ago, and there's not one day I don't cry for him."

I struggled to hold back my own tears. "I know how you feel. May I pray for you?"

"No, I don't need prayers." Anger rang in her voice. "Will prayers bring my son back?"

I leaned back, and she continued sobbing. A lump pressed against my throat. Silently, I asked, *Lord, how can this poor woman make it without You?*

The program finally began with the leader welcoming participants. Parents joined hands in a circle with lit candles in the middle, each representing the child they'd lost. One by one, the parents took turns saying something about their child.

On the way home, I turned to Gene. "I don't think I want to go back. All those parents crying breaks my heart."

"I didn't feel encouraged either," he agreed.

Once home, I sat at the computer and opened a file that contained books of the Bible. After listening to a few chapters from Psalms, I opened another file that contained my journal. That night I wrote:

Father, I just observed how other parents face the loss of their child. My heart aches for them. The peace You gave me is supernatural. I don't know why You placed in me a desire to let these other parents know about the peace they, too, could have. I truly, truly don't pretend to know how to help others. I don't even know where to begin to speak to their pain. But you can. Would you use me? There must be thousands of parents who are drowning in their grief because of the emptiness their child left. I could be too, but though I cannot understand how or why, my heart is filled with the presence of Your grace, the peace only You can give, and the hope I can't do without.

If I were to ask You something right now, it would be for You to open the door for me to be a testimony of Your healing hand, restoring power and guidance through the dark valley of heartache. I'm willing, Lord, and ready to go through the doors You open. Inside me is a longing to help parents feel Your love, receive Your comfort, and hear Your words of constant compassion. You have changed my sorrow to gratitude, and I am so grateful, Lord, for the guarantee I'll see Joe again. I'm grateful for the way You whisper comfort during the dark nights. How You repeat Your promises of healing. Thank you, Lord, for drying my tears and removing my fears.

In the days that followed, I turned my focus to Jason and Jeff. How were they handling the tragedy of losing their younger brother? As I was praying for God to show me how to help them, a young woman Jason was dating, Rachel, called to check up on us. She shared, "Jason and I were just talking about Joe being in heaven and having eternal life because he'd accepted Christ as his Savior."

A fine Christian young woman of deep faith, Rachel would in time become Jason's wife and our first of two precious daughters-in-law. She went on to give more details. She and Jason had been driving when they had the conversation. As soon as Jason heard Rachel's explanation, he turned down the volume on the radio. "Wait a minute! How come I didn't know any of this?"

Jason had learned about Jesus through attending Catholic churches and schools. But he'd never really heard the full plan of salvation since he wasn't living at home with us when we started attending South Orlando Baptist. Nor had he been exposed to Christian youth ministry or Bible studies as Jeff and Joe had. I'd often encouraged him to come to church with us and tried to explain the way of salvation to him. Although he'd dismissed our invitations, I'd prayed constantly for God to touch his heart.

But now after hearing the plan of salvation from Rachel, Jason invited Jesus into his life. A beautiful transformation took place in his heart. He began studying the Bible and joined a solid Bible-believing church. The next thing I knew, Jason was on fire for Jesus. Like a racehorse taking off when the gate is opened, his commitment to spread the gospel became bold and passionate.

In contrast, Jeff kept his feelings inside, though he was probably the one who missed Joe the most since they'd done everything together—sports, camps, youth activities, and social functions. I poured out my heart to God. *Lord, only you can ease my Jeff's pain. Only you can show him the path to healing.*

As more weeks passed by, my parents eventually turned their talk from the sadness they felt to good memories of all the silly, fun things Joe used to do. The time was right for me to finish the book I was writing. In its pages, I related how my season of sorrow turned to acceptance, then to peace, then to gratitude.

Finishing the manuscript, I printed it. With some hesitation, I walked into the family room where Gene was sitting. "Here. Would you like to read this?"

I'd battled about including the infidelity episode, not just because Gene might feel uncomfortable, but I also wanted to avoid offending God in any way through sharing such intimate details. I heard Gene turn page after page. He continued the next day. When he'd finished, he came to my desk and set down the manuscript. "I'm done."

"Are you okay with me writing all the details of what happened to us?" I asked.

Gene sighed. "If it helps other couples, I think you should include it all."

I could hear sincerity in his voice. We ended up publishing the completed manuscript. My thought had been that someday far into the future, my grandkids would read how God weaves His love through someone's life journey and trials. But it turned out my grandchildren wouldn't be the only ones touched. I was amazed and humbled by the sheer volume of feedback we received. The internet provided an effective way for me to make contacts and be invited as a guest on media outlets reaching audiences globally. Emails poured in from Germany, England, and Australia, as well as across North America. All shared how my story of suffering turned to triumph had touched them.

One woman from Mexico wrote: "My husband saw me reading your book, and he also saw me crying in some chapters. He isn't a reader, but he asked to read the book. When he finished it, he came to me, got on his knees, and said, 'If I put you through what Janet's husband put her through, please forgive me.'"

She went on to share how she and her husband had attended church together for the first time. Letters like this one stunned me. Clearly, God was directing my path. But where would He lead me next? What would His plans include?

His answer came one evening after our women's Bible study. I was there with a friend. Once we'd finished the session, I took my friend's arm, and we walked out. As we did so, she said to me, "You need to share your story with our group."

I laughed. "What story?"

"About how you came to the United States and how God helped you when you lost your sight and how He was with you when Joe was killed."

I smiled. "Girlfriend, that's all in the book."

"Nope, you need to give your testimony in person, not just in writing."

Give my testimony? My story is really God's testimony of His goodness at work. But sharing those painful episodes before a group would require a different kind of courage. I'd have to wait for God to grant that to me.

The next day, I read about Moses and his hesitation about going back to Egypt to bring the Israelites out. He tried to make excuses, but God won. Later when Joshua faced his fears about leading God's people across the Jordan, God commanded him to have courage. And when Elijah fell, exhausted with discouragement and fear, after his big showdown with the prophets of Baal on Mount Carmel, God provided what he needed for strength.

The message God was sending me was clear. But I wasn't one of these giants of faith in the Bible. I was just a blind *chica* from Bolivia totally devoted to Christ Jesus, and completely enveloped in His love. That night I journaled:

Father, I don't know if I should laugh at the notion that I should be speaking to groups, sharing what happened to me. But I do know You have taken me places I never dreamed. You have given me strength to bring down barriers. You lifted me from dark valleys and took me to mountaintops. So, if this is Your way to give me the desires of my heart, I need the courage only You can give, I need Your wisdom, and I need a clear signal this is from You.

His signal came. After our next women's Bible study, my friend stood and addressed the group. "Hey, I have a request. I've been thinking that Janet should share her story with us. She's never done that before, and I think we need to hear it."

The other women clapped. "Yes, yes, we want to hear it."

They placed a flimsy metal podium in the front of the room, and I stood behind it, trying to gather my thoughts. I'd been interviewed on radio and television back when my sons were small. But that was as spokeswoman for our moms organization. Relating my own story in front of a live group made me break out in a sweat.

Finally, I began, stuttering a bit, hesitating in certain places, and with a few tears when I related the experience of losing Joe. I confessed to those ladies that I'd been spiritually blind when I had sight and now God had allowed me to see my life so beautifully.

After I finished, one of them hugged me tight and whispered in my ear, "Thank you so much. My husband wants a divorce, no one knows, and I'm a mess. I needed to hear your story."

When I finally got to bed that night, sleep eluded me. It was too late to get up and journal, so I simply lifted my thoughts heavenward in prayer. *Lord, I'm in awe at the way You guide me through foreign territory and the supernatural way in which You remove my fears. Thank you, thank you, thank you.*

Little did I know that God was about to show me this was only the beginning.

CHAPTER TWENTY-SEVEN
EXPANDING MY WINGS

He said to them, "Go into all the world and preach the good news to all creation."

—Mark 16:15

I stirred a bowl of banana bread batter as I chatted with my Bible study friend on speaker phone. "I wish I'd done a better job sharing my story last week."

"You're too hard on yourself," she responded firmly. "After all, that was your first time. And everyone was touched. In fact, some even had tears in their eyes."

Whether interpreting, training, or writing, giving my best to everything I do has always been the desire of my heart. I resolved to do the same with speaking. A friend suggested I join Toastmasters, a local group that helps people polish their public speaking skills. My parents were happy to drive me, and they always relished seeing me come out with blue ribbons that indicated I'd won first place. Toastmasters is where I learned about organizing speeches, openings, props, humor, closing, and storytelling.

Local Rotary Clubs, where professionals network and encourage each other, became my first audience. Encouraged by their feedback, I scheduled speaking engagements with Chamber of Commerce organizations as well. After each presentation, more opportunities to speak followed. When I spoke to local Christian women's groups, I added the gospel.

Word of mouth became my best marketing tool. As invitations flooded in, audiences purchased copies of my book. After speaking events, men and women both approached me to say, "When I came here, I thought I had problems and was feeling so discouraged. But after hearing what God did for you, I know He can do the same for me. I have more hope and feel like a new person."

I'm not sure which was greater—my amazement or my gratitude. God had once again demonstrated that with Him there is no blindness, only the full vision of His grace. But I also needed God's wisdom because Gene and I were facing another conflict. One day, his secretary at Disney World called. "Janet, Gene isn't thinking of leaving his job, is he?"

I swallowed hard. I wanted to sound reassuring, but Gene had briefly mentioned to me his intentions of starting his own business. I finally said, "If it were up to me, he certainly won't be leaving. I know the next step is VP, and everyone says he's doing so well. So that would seem a logical next goal for him."

"That's right." Her tone sounded almost pleading. "Everyone loves him here."

I loved Gene too, but his decisions were confusing to me. Leaving a position where he excelled and that provided income beyond our dreams just didn't make sense. But no matter what reasoning I presented, Gene's response was the same. "I need to at least try and see if I can make it on my own. I'll start with opening a few retail stores, then see how it goes."

So, Gene left Disney. His initial success with the first retail store he opened made me think he had a good plan. But when the 2008 change of the economy came, the business lost money. The next venture suffered fraud and theft. Each subsequent venture seemed to fail as well.

One evening, I walked into Gene's home office. "I don't know where all this is leading, but I'm really worried about these businesses. I think you need to consider applying for a job."

"Trust me," he said. "I'll work all this out."

I'd heard that before. And the last time it had ended in bankruptcy and massive debt. Silently, I prayed, *Lord, show me how to be a submissive wife. It's so hard when I see wrong decisions and our financial problems increasing.*

In the meantime, I pressed on with my own interpreting job. I also wrote articles for publication and accepted every opportunity to speak. One of those opportunities tested my faith. I received an email inviting me to speak in North Carolina. Gulp! I'd have to fly from Orlando to that church.

"Do you want me to go with you?" Gene asked.

That could have been the answer to assuage my fear of traveling alone. But I couldn't rely on Gene taking time from juggling his businesses each time I needed to fly somewhere. The reality was that even when I was sighted, I'd never traveled alone to an unfamiliar place. I'd never stayed in a hotel room alone either. The thought of both experiences made my stomach cramp. That was the moment when a verse from God's Word I'd engraved in my heart came alive.

For God has not given us a spirit of fear, but of power and of love and of a sound mind. (2 Timothy 1:7, NKJV)

If those three gifts of power, love, and a sound mind were what God promised, why wouldn't I take them? The first one I needed to apply was sound mind. In other words, use wisdom to plan ahead and take necessary steps to make sure I had someone to meet me at my destination. Calling the airline as I did when I traveled to Bolivia some years back, I requested an escort to help me navigate through the airport. Next was the gift of power. God's power at work in me to bring success and defeat any opposition or potential danger. The third gift was God's love. I wouldn't be alone in the hotel room, God's love would surround me providing reassurance, companionship, and peace.

With all those gifts safely tucked in my heart, fear turned to sweet anticipation of adventure. I was ready.

Mom walked into my closet. "Let me help you pack."

Taking her tiny, thin hands in mine, I steered her to a stool. "Sit here. If you help me, I won't know where things are in my suitcase. I need to do it myself so I know what I'm packing and where everything is."

Fun moments between speaking engagements.

She sighed. "Okay, but I just don't know about you traveling alone with no family to wait for you or relatives to stay with. What if something happens?"

I smiled. "Where do you think I could go that God wouldn't be?"

"Oh, honey!" She hugged me tight, "You are so brave. I don't know what I'd do if anything happened to you."

I winked at her. "The only thing that could happen is that more people would know about Jesus. And maybe then they'd learn to walk by faith, not by sight."

All fell into place. During the twelve years I'd been working as an interpreter, I'd accumulated many vacation days that allowed me to travel. As invitations to speak continued to pour in, flying to various states became an entertaining and adventurous activity. The routine seldom changed. Gene dropped me off at the curbside counter and kissed me goodbye. From then on, an escort guided me through security and on to my gate. Boarding the plane also became simple with the help of airline personnel.

Each trip presented a bit of humor. On one occasion, a kind flight attendant led me to my seat down the narrow airplane aisle. "Your seat is to your right."

I grabbed the seat to brace myself. "Thank you."

As I slipped in, I noticed that what I'd gripped so tightly began to move. Only then did I realize that instead of gripping the seat, I'd grabbed a bald man's head. I smile as I write this because those embarrassing moments didn't discourage my travels. On the contrary, they served to enrich my speaking with more stories.

Without fail, I made new friends in airports, on the plane, and at the hotel. Once I reached my destination, an escort always awaited me as I exited the plane. Holding the escort's arm, I headed to the baggage claim, then to the airport exit. That's where I met the person assigned to the speaker. She would drive me to the hotel and walk me to my room. Before she left me there, I always asked, "Would you do me a favor? Could you make sure all the lights are off?"

Most of my guides hesitated. Others asked, "Are you sure?"

"Yup, I can't tell if they're on or off." Leaning toward my guide, I whispered, "It's not good to sleep with the lights on."

This always drew a chuckle. Once alone in the hotel room, I used my fingertips to feel the location of the furniture, the lay out of the bedroom and bathroom. Next, I unpacked my suitcase and arranged everything in order. The next morning, showering, dressing, makeup, and hair were done with ease. With each trip, I became more comfortable traveling alone and speaking to large and small audiences.

Although each experience was exciting and always rewarding, sometimes draining, it was nice to be home again. But this time, I didn't expect what awaited me at my arrival.

CHAPTER TWENTY-EIGHT
FORGIVENESS

As the heavens are higher than the earth, so are my ways higher
than your ways and my thoughts than your thoughts.

—Isaiah 55:9

As Gene picked me up at the airport we exchanged our usual
affectionate greetings, but his demeanor was solemn. I turned
to him. "Well, anything interesting happen while I was gone?"

"Not really." He paused, then cleared his throat. "We got the
letter from the district attorney."

I knew what that meant. I pressed my head back on the seat and
inhaled a deep breath. We expected this next step to arrive one day,
but I still wasn't prepared.

The letter informed us that the trial to prosecute the man who
had killed our son Joe had been scheduled. The trial would begin
on October 27th, which also happened to be my birthday.

My heart sank. Though I'd known this step was inevitable, I'd tried to push it out of my mind. Now a sudden drain of energy swept over me as I reviewed what had happened that night. Once home, I sat for a while in silence. Then I went to my computer, opened my journal, and wrote:

It's a dark day today, Lord. I knew this would be upon us, but I'm not prepared. I'm not sure I even want to be present in that courtroom. The trial is necessary as the man has to be punished. But I feel we're the ones being punished as well by having to relive what happened that night. I need Your strength. I need Your power to defeat the attacks of anxiety and fear. I need Your loving arms around me. I'm boldly asking for supernatural strength for my sons, husband, and family. Don't let me surrender to anguish. This trial is in Your hands, and the results are in Your will.

The trial lasted three long days. Each witness presented details of that night. The way Joe and his friend had entered a 7-11 parking lot in his Jeep. Then the other man pulled in. My Joe wasn't aware the man was armed with a knife. He stabbed Joe twenty-three times and Joe's friend seven times. Joe's friend survived, but the attack took Joe's life.

My heartache grew as we endured the medical forensics report describing each of Joe's stab wounds, including one to his heart. Holding on to Gene, I silently cried out to God, *I need you, Lord! I desperately need you.*

At the end of the third day, the jury was ready with the verdict. We all stood as the jury foreman stepped to the front. My heart raced and I could hardly breathe as the silence in the courtroom was broken by the jury foreman's voice. He read the verdict. "We the jury find the defendant not guilty of all counts."

Our side of the courtroom gasped. The other side cheered. The killer's attorney had built a case of self-defense based on Florida's lenient "stand your ground" law, claiming the confrontation had been a mutual fight with one combatant defending himself against two. It didn't matter that Joe and his friend were unarmed and the killer had somehow landed a total of thirty stab wounds without suffering any injuries. The man went home free while we went home destroyed.

Our first task was to calm Jason and Jeff as well as Joe's friends. They displayed anger and spoke of vengeance. Gene called them together in the hallway outside the courtroom. "All of you, nothing you do will bring Joe back. If you cause any trouble, the only ones who will suffer will be our family."

We drove home in a dark cloud of disbelief. I couldn't speak. I couldn't even cry. What I felt wasn't sorrow, anger, or disappointment. Doubt is what attacked me. Forcing myself to sit at the computer, I journaled:

Lord, You were in that courtroom. You heard the details. You heard every word. I trusted You. I counted on Your justice and Your love to make sure Joe's killer received what he deserved. You promise in Your Word that You will deliver

us from all our troubles. Why, then, did Your promise fail us?
How do we move forward? How do I share with audiences
about Your faithfulness if it wasn't there when we needed it
most? Still, even though my heart is shattered, I choose, Lord,
to believe in You. Though my energy fails me, I will not doubt
that one day You will show me the other side of this injustice.
I have to lean on You, Lord. I have no one else.

That night, Gene and I followed our usual bedtime routine in silence, but we didn't miss our prayer time. Kneeling at the foot of our bed, we asked God to help us understand this injustice. Our prayers were genuine, and with each passing day, our peace gradually returned. Finally, one night, we were able to talk about the man responsible for Joe's death and his future. Though he hadn't served one day in prison, he would have to be accountable to God, not to us.

That said, we too would be accountable to God if we continued to hold resentment, anger, or animosity against this man. The only step God required from us was to extend forgiveness.

That night we chose to forgive the man who had killed our Joe. We weren't able to tell him in person since we had no idea where he might be. But our total and genuine forgiveness for what he'd done removed the bars of resentment and anger that could have held us prisoners. That night of forgiveness we flew out of our dark prison into the sunshine of God's freedom.

Forgiveness also allowed us to welcome more fully the radiance of God's love. A love that filled us even when we didn't understand the seeming injustice. A love that conquers grief. A love that turns all things to good. I realized that God had indeed kept His promises. He'd never abandoned us. He'd been faithful in turning injustice to good since in no other way could Gene and I be tasting the sweet freedom of forgiveness.

Could this downpour of unexpected blessings continue?

CHAPTER TWENTY-NINE
TREASURES FROM THE HEART

Now to him who is able to do immeasurably more than all we ask
or imagine, according to his power that is at work within us.

—Ephesians 3:20

*L*ord, how do I know what to share with the public? Should I be
private about my pain? Should I keep the details of injustice to
myself? What details will glorify you, and which should be kept
personal?

Even before I received an answer to those questions, I stood
behind the podium at a women's conference in California, striving
to defeat doubt with the courage David displayed when he brought
down Goliath. One by one, I shared the ups and downs of my life.
This time I added the trial, injustice, and our choice to forgive.
When I stepped off the stage, a woman hugged me. "I needed to hear
that. I've held so much unforgiveness against the man who

molested me. I knew I had to forgive. I just didn't know how. Now I do. Thank you."

That's when God showed me His purpose in this injustice and all the pain we had suffered. He also showed me His plan to touch others in their own unforgiveness by turning my speaking and writing into a non-profit ministry. With Gene's help, JC Empowerment Ministries was born.

One Sunday morning after the worship service, one of our pastors asked me to step into his office. "We want you to pray about a task we'd like you to undertake. If God leads you, we'd like you to teach the women's Sunday school class."

I gave a beaming smile. "I will pray, and I hope God says yes."

He did. Teaching that class Sunday after Sunday made God's Word come alive with delightful clarity. And how rewarding to witness the spiritual growth of those precious ladies. My teaching duties expanded when Jason and Rachel enriched our lives with our first granddaughter. I vowed that I'd be the one to teach her everything about Jesus.

One Saturday evening, Jason carried her in his arms as he walked in our front door. "Here she is to spend time with her Nana."

I extended my arms toward my granddaughter. "I gotcha, sweet baby."

Setting her down, I pinned tiny jingle bells to the back of her shirt so I could keep track of her. That became our routine. When she came in the front door on her own, I heard the tap, tap, tap of her tiny steps as she dashed into my arms. She would then turn her back toward me, waiting for me to pin on those bells.

Jason chuckled at my silly way to care for her. "You're amazing, Mom. She's learning so much from you. And so am I."

"God always makes a way for us to do anything," I responded, "so as long as we choose to see every situation through His eyes."

He sighed. "I know. My side vision is beginning to decrease. But I don't worry about it. Look at all you've accomplished. With or without sight, I'll be okay."

"You'll be more than okay," I assured him vehemently. "God has a mighty and wonderful plan for your life."

I prayed fervently over him in faith that God would grant him full physical and spiritual vision all the days of his life. In the meantime, I concentrated on teaching my granddaughter to see with her heart. She was already learning. Picking up a toy, she placed it in my hand. "Here, Nana, can you feel it? It's my frog."

Janet with her grandkids.

Taking my other hand, she placed my fingertips on the frog's face. "See? These are his eyes."

"Funny looking eyes," I teased her.

Since I couldn't read her books, I made up stories, dramatizing them as I related them to her. Each had a message that pointed to Jesus. When her little brother came along two years later, I did the same with him. Through the years that followed, I told stories not only to them but to countless other audiences

With God's Word alive in me and the Holy Spirit as my companion, I picked up the white cane of courage and ventured forth to impart my message to an ever-expanding territory across the United States, Cuba, the Caribbean, South America, Mexico, and the Philippines. God proved over and over again that pain has no borders, anguish has no unique language, and devastation has no ethnicity. What all these people in so many distant places and time zones had in common was the way God restores those who call upon Him. How God heals those who believe. And no matter what corner of the world, God turns all things good for those who truly love Him.

Each group I visited fueled my writing. When I wasn't interpreting on the phone, my fingers danced on the keyboard as I submitted inspirational articles and stories to local newspapers, Christian and secular print and online magazines, as well as national publications such as *Chicken Soup for the Soul*. At first, I received rejections. Eventually, most of my writing was accepted.

One day, Mom and I were sitting in the dental office waiting room when she suddenly jumped up from her chair. Pushing a magazine into my hands, she exclaimed, "You won't believe what I found in the stack of magazines on this table. It's *Guidepost*. And your picture is on the cover. I wonder if they'd let me take it home."

I shook my head. "We don't have to do that, Mom. They sent us free copies when it first came out, don't you remember?"

She probably didn't since that particular *Guidepost* issue was one of many magazines and anthologies by then where my writing had appeared. A cover picture was far less common. Framing, filing, and displaying everything I wrote or accomplished became a passion for Mom. One afternoon, she took a visiting friend by the hand and pointed to the bookshelf beside the fireplace. "See all these? They're all *Chicken Soup for the Soul* books. There are thirty-two of them, and each one has a story from my Janet."

As years swept by, Mom was equally proud when my second, third, and fourth book titles were released. She giggled like a little girl when the first copies of each new book came in the mail. She loved to arrange each on the bookshelf and tell everyone about them. But her tears flowed when a newly printed Spanish-language devotional Bible for women arrived that featured a selection from my second book, *Simply Salsa*.

One of Mom's favorite tasks was to welcome media teams to our home. Over the years, local television hosts and camera crews from regional, national, and international programs came to the house to interview me. Mom would sit patiently on a chair facing the bay window that looked out onto our front driveway. As soon as the media vans pulled in, she would dash toward me, her voice getting higher with excitement. "They're here! It's *The 700 Club*. Quick, let me check your makeup."

Janet and her Mom, Ita.

Once we received the date and time each interview was scheduled to air, Mom got busy calling on the phone or writing emails to invite family and friends in other states, Bolivia, even her friends in Israel, to watch.

I continued to juggle my full-time job and writing with speaking engagements and conferences. Each opportunity sparked excitement and challenged me to deliver a powerful message that would inspire and empower audiences. But in the secret compartment of my heart, old insecurities raised their heads, especially when I found myself sharing the stage with speakers I considered way above my league such as Lee Strobel, John C. Maxwell, Pricilla Shirer, and Gov. Mike Huckabee.

I gained confidence from God's sweet whisper to my heart, "With me, there are no leagues, only the love I've placed in you to share with the world."

As God provided opportunities for more writing and speaking, He also brought new surprises in my interpreting career. One national conference sponsored by my employer culminated in an awards banquet. My taste buds were having a party with the delicious dessert, so I wasn't paying attention as the MC listed the admirable accomplishments of the person receiving that year's most prestigious award of Professional Excellence.

Suddenly, I nearly choked on my dessert as I heard my name. In the past, that award had been given to truly stellar executives and professionals. And now to me? I was overwhelmed with shock and gratitude. As a friend walked me to the stage, I heard a thunderous applause.

"Just so you know," she whispered, "they're giving you a standing ovation."

I flew home that night and gave the good news to Gene and my parents. Then I headed to the computer and journaled:

Father, thank you isn't enough. The journey You've ushered me through couldn't be found in the most creative fairy tales. When You brought us from Bolivia, we thought our dreams had come true. But You had Your own dream for my life. One that turned my blindness to a beautiful portrait only faith can see. You lifted me from despair and turned tragedies into victorious triumphs. You showed me justice through the beauty of forgiveness. And now You've proved once again that Your promises of life full and abundant are so vibrant and real.

If I could, I would have frozen this season of my life so it would endure forever.

CHAPTER THIRTY
THE OTHER SIDE OF DESPAIR

He fulfills the desires of those who fear him; he hears their cry and saves them.

—Psalm 145:19

Like the pages of my books, the seasons of my life turned with each passing year. The ministry God entrusted to me grew. So did my grandchildren. Jason and Rachel's son and daughter were about to reach their teen years. Jeff was also now married to a wonderful young woman named Krystal. My passion and devotion to serve God continued to increase.

But my perseverance was about to be tested once again. During these past years when I'd been focused on an ever-expanding ministry along with a full-time job, Gene had been focused on more and more business ventures ranging from retail to real estate. One morning as I got ready to begin my interpreting shift, I asked Gene,

"What's going on? You seem stressed. Are you still having trouble with those property sales?"

"I've just got a lot on my mind," he responded curtly. "The issues with the business are making me anxious. I didn't sleep last night either."

I resisted the urge to remind him how I'd opposed getting into that business. Blaming him would only cause more anxiety. What concerned me more was his aloof demeanor.

"What can I do to help?" I asked.

"Nothing," he mumbled. "Nothing at all."

Leaving the room, he closed the door behind him. As the following weeks passed, our conversations centered on the superficial. Though we didn't argue or have confrontations of any kind, a gloomy darkness hovered over us. While I interpreted on the phone, Gene spent long hours in his office at home. Our prayer times together also diminished. Though Gene never refused to pray with me, God's peace seemed to elude him.

We still attended Sunday services together at the Baptist church we'd both grown to love. While I taught women's Sunday school, Gene used his accounting skills to help on the financial committee and sometimes led the men's group.

Meanwhile, a different kind of challenge had surfaced at home. Though Mom and I had tried to persuade him, my father had refused any conventional treatment for his prostate problems. Eventually, these turned into cancer.

Mom came to my room during one of my work breaks. "I'm worried about your father. He has me read the scale each time he weighs himself. He has lost fifteen pounds already."

Trying to convince my father to see a specialist or follow any treatment only triggered angry refusals. As months went by, he seemed healthy, alert, and active. But his continued weight loss concerned all of us. My heart and mind were heavy with worry for him.

And for Gene as he faced his own emotional cancer. One evening, Gene came downstairs from his office, his voice low and somber as he admitted, "I think I need some help. I'm going to get some counseling."

Weeks of counseling turned to months and then a full year. I looked for changes, for hope, for solutions. But the old Gene, who always had a kind demeanor and positive, loving words, seemed lost in a gloomy silence. He finally came to me, his tone defeated. "I've decided I need to work on this on my own. I'll be moving out just for a while."

I gasped. A while? What did that even mean? Were we separating? Where would he go? To my mind, we were together for better or for worse. This was the worse we'd gone through since his previous infidelity all those decades before when he hadn't yet placed his faith in Jesus. And once again, his choices threatened our marriage.

I chose my words carefully. "I hate this as much as you do. But I'm willing to support you. And I'll pray even more now."

With Gene gone, I asked friends for rides to church. My requests for prayer for him became more frequent. Everyone at church asked about him. They wondered how he was, where he was, when he would be coming back. Questions for which I had no answers.

One afternoon, Mom came into my bedroom. "Is everything okay? Where's Gene? Still out of town?"

She had to know. But what explanation could I give her about the emotional chaos that disturbed Gene? I inhaled deeply as I reached for her hand. "Gene's going to be away for a while. He has some things to sort out. But we'll be okay. There's nothing you should worry about."

Father seemed to be improving. He even asked to go to his favorite restaurant. Mom and I took him, but he hardly touched his favorite dish we ordered for him.

Sometimes Gene would call. "Do you need me to come back and help?"

Of course, I wanted him to come back, but his healing was more important. "We're doing okay."

I bit my lip to keep from screaming out my frustration. As the weeks past, Father grew weaker. He slept more and stayed in bed most of the day. Eventually, his legs couldn't hold him up. When he fell, I called the paramedics for help. Mom and I knew it was time. I contacted a doctor, relaying my father's symptoms and diagnosis. Without hesitation, the doctor approved hospice. In a matter of two weeks, Father entered the glory of heaven.

My brother Ed and his wife came to help the last few days. This eased our load, but the loss of my father along with Gene's absence sent me into a tornado of dark emotions. In the silence of night, questions bombarded my mind. Would I ever overcome my pain? God's Word again whispered to me.

In this world you will have trouble. But take heart! I have overcome the world. (John 16:33)

Yes, this world was filled with painful troubles. But my Savior had overcome them all, and He would overcome the troubles in my world too. I put my faith to work and engraved that promise in my soul.

One morning, I woke up and headed to the kitchen for a drink of water. My mom's embrace startled me as I had no idea she was there. She said tenderly, "Your eyes are all red and swollen. Don't cry, honey. Your father's in heaven where we all want to be."

She had no idea my heart wasn't just aching for my father but for Gene and the emotional and mental troubles tormenting him. The longer Gene was gone, the more serious our separation seemed. I clung to one of God's promises that had become especially meaningful to me.

The Lord is close to the brokenhearted and saves those who are crushed in spirit. (Psalm 34:18)

I knew God was near and that He would never abandon us, but sometimes loneliness added to my grief. I called a dear friend and shared my heart with her. She gave me wise, loving advice. "Sometimes we can't fix the darkness that someone else carries. All we can do is turn it over to God."

"I know," I sighed. "I have to keep God's truth from getting lost in the craziness of this mess."

Life had to go on. My attention turned to reassuring Mom that all was under control. Arrangements for the headstone. Delivery of the urn. Insurance claims. Bank issues. Night after night, I dragged myself to bed, exhausted. Instead of sleeping, I journaled:

Lord, losing Father on top of this heartache with Gene is sending me in a spiral to the darkness of despair. Yet with everything in me, I will believe, truly believe, that Your watchful eye is upon Gene and upon me. I will repeat over and over again the power of Your healing. I will always put my hope in You and You alone. I will boldly believe someday You'll turn all this to good.

A few weeks later, I had returned to my interpreting work when Gene called to say apologetically, "I'm so sorry you have to go through all this on your own. I'm so sorry for leaving when I did. But my own issues are too deep right now."

Words of understanding eluded me, and I hated that tears flowed each time I spoke to him on the phone. I managed to respond calmly, "I'm praying my way through all this."

One thing was certain. The battle Gene faced was bigger than both of us. *Lord, where will this end up?* I prayed desperately. *Only You can touch Gene's heart. Only You can mend the wounds and heal the scars he carries.*

I was willing to help my husband carry his cross no matter how long it took. But Gene had made his decision. Late one night, he called again, his voice despondent and sad. "I've been thinking. I can't leave you in limbo. You need to move on with your life."

My life? It was supposed to be our lives, our issues we needed to work out together. My mouth became dry. "What are you telling me?"

"I'm sorry I betrayed you this way. I think for both of us a divorce is the only answer. I'll take my name off the house. I've prepared a budget. You'll have enough for all the bills."

Divorce? The word sent chills through me. Not in my worst nightmares had divorce ever been an option for us. As he continued speaking, I held back words that would have blasted him with my shock, anger, and grief. I finally pressed the button to hang up. *That's it? Just like that, forty-two years of marriage is over?*

Dropping to my knees, I cried out in anguish, *Lord, this can't be happening! I'll never understand this kind of betrayal. The darkness I see in him is killing me. I have to trust that You'll hold me up because right now I don't think I have the strength to breathe or face my world.*

My desperation didn't wane. Instead, it forced me to once again lift my thoughts to God's promises. I had no control over Gene's emotional turmoil, but I could control my own sorrow and grief. I'd experienced similar anguish in the emergency room nearly eighteen years ago when Joe had entered heaven. God had promised me peace, and He'd given it to me. He'd declared triumph in my life, and He'd kept that promise. He'd whispered reassurance for my tomorrows, and He'd made that happen.

And I had no reason to doubt He'd do the same now. My sorrow for Gene was now in God's hands. His future would be under God's watchful eyes. His restoration would come wrapped in God's grace and boundless love. And I had already made my own choice of forgiveness.

Which didn't make the days and weeks and months that followed easy ones. But with each tear I shed, God was attentive. In each anxious moment, His presence was with me. And into my devastation, He was about to pour another dose of restoring love.

Chapter Thirty-One
Unprepared for Loneliness

And without faith it is impossible to please God, because anyone
who comes to him must believe that he exists and that he rewards
those who earnestly seek him.

—Hebrews 11:6

D ivorce. I hated that word. God hates it too (see Malachi 2:16).
Just two months later with my heart sorrowing for Gene and
crushed under my crumbled marriage, we signed the divorce papers.

How do I move on after forty-two years of marriage? How do I
face our sons and my mom? Everyone at church, in our family, and
among our friends assumed we had a happy, healthy marriage.
Now I was in a foreign territory as a divorced woman. Something
I'd never even imagined could happen to us after all we'd overcome
and after receiving blessing upon blessing from God. Was it my
fault for failing to recognize the demons Gene was battling?

I had no answers. Instead, my own battle to move forward began. In the midst of the unknown, fear gripped me. My loneliness ached for the presence of the Lord, and my emptiness longed for God's Word to brush my soul. As I listened to familiar promises in Scripture, God wrapped me in the warmth of His love.

So do not fear, for I am with you; do not be dismayed, for I am your God. I will strengthen you and help you, I will uphold you with my righteous right hand. (Isaiah 41:10)

I prayed. *I do receive Your strength, Lord. I will depend on Your hand to lift me up. With all I have in me, I will rely on Your presence to be right beside me.*

I called Jason, and together we conferenced Jeff in a three-way call. I took a deep breath to gather courage, then said quietly, "Guys, you know Dad has been gone for a year. Yesterday, we both signed the divorce papers."

There was a brief silence. Then Jason asked, "Mom, are you okay?"

Tears burned my eyes. "Honey, I am."

"I was hoping this wouldn't have to happen," Jeff said. "But we respect your decision. What can we do, Mom? Do you need anything at all?"

Their loving, kind reaction soothed my heart with a sweetness I hadn't felt in a long time. Now I had to let my mom know. I struggled how to tell her as I wanted to protect her from any heartache. One day after my work shift, I settled on the couch in her sitting area.

Swallowing the lump in my throat, I said, "I don't want you to worry, but Gene will be gone for a while. He's going through some painful issues. In fact, he thinks divorce is best for us."

"Oh, no!" Hugging me, Mom burst into tears. "What happened?"

"Too many things." I handed her a tissue. "But you know what? You and I and the Lord will be just fine. Has He ever abandoned us?"

"No," she said between sobs.

"Well, He won't abandon us now either. We'll be okay. We have each other, and God is our father and husband now."

During the day, I tried to keep Mom occupied by allowing her to do the cooking for both of us. Her favorite pastime was listening to the dramatized Bible and sometimes to David Jeremiah's teachings. After she went to bed, I spent sleepless nights listening to praise music and Christian teachings. As I lay there mourning for my marriage, God knew just what to say.

Forget the former things, do not dwell on the past. See, I am doing a new thing! Now it springs up, do you not perceive it? I am making a way in the desert and streams in the wasteland. (Isaiah 43:18-19)

While I didn't yet perceive the good things God was doing, I chose without hesitation to erase any trace of resentment or guilt from the wasteland of my heart. Moment by moment, the veil of gloom parted, and I welcomed the streams of blessings into the desert of my pain.

With my father gone, Mom and I now shopped for groceries together. She drove to the store and quickly found the first scooter available. She became a pro at starting them and taking off. The grocery aisles became her racetrack while I held on to the back of the seat, occasionally having to jog a little to keep up.

The time came when we decided we needed to change our Sunday routine. For many years, Gene and I had worshipped at our

Baptist church while Mom and my father attended Catholic Mass. One Saturday afternoon, I asked Mom, "Do you want me to go with you to Mass tomorrow?"

"Actually," she responded, "I've been wanting for a long time now to attend a church where they teach the Bible."

I smiled widely. "Then how about if we find one that's close to home. I know an excellent church nearby we can visit, and you can tell me if you like it."

Stepping into that new church was a fresh start for both of us. The greeters touched Mom's heart with their warm words and welcoming kindness. After the service, I held her arm as we walked out. Once in the car, she gushed about her experience. "I never heard such a wonderful message, so clear, so true."

From then on, we attended there as our home church. I liked the fact that no one in the congregation knew I was an author or a speaker. No one knew I'd taught Sunday school. Best of all, no one asked questions about Gene or details about what was going on.

But it didn't take long for the pastor to learn of my previous ministry. As Mom and I exited from a Sunday morning service, he stopped us. "Ms. Janet, I understand you're an author and speaker."

I nodded. "Only through God's grace."

"I'd like to talk with you. Could you make an appointment with the church secretary?"

I grinned. "I sure can."

A few days later, I met with the pastor in his office, where I shared all the details of my journey and the ministry God had given me. To my surprise, he invited me to be a guest speaker at all four services the church held each Sunday. The invitation was a blessing. But was I ready? Was my heart healed enough? Would my message still carry the power of God's restoration?

"Can I get back to you with the answer?" I responded.

I had a few months to prepare. But I battled with doubt as to my ability to stand at the pulpit again. Over the past fifteen years of speaking, God had granted me His favor to deliver with confidence, poise, clarity, and creativity messages He'd used to change hearts and transform souls. Had all those abilities sunk into the mud of my tribulations? For the past year, I'd politely declined all speaking invitations. Was I ready to inspire congregations again when my own heart still bled?

God was about to answer that question. One day, after one of my interpreting sessions, our home phone rang. When I answered, the words I heard caught me off guard. Leaning forward in my chair, I demanded with stunned astonishment, "Excuse me, what did you say? Could you repeat that?"

"I said that the leadership committee of the Central Florida Hispanic Chamber of Commerce has chosen you as the 2019 Don Quixote Lifetime Achievement Award winner," the caller repeated patiently.

I couldn't speak. This prestigious award had been presented to such illustrious Hispanics as the first Latina surgeon general under the George Bush presidential administration. The list of men and women who had received this once-in-a-lifetime award all occupied high positions way beyond my league. Did I deserve this incredible recognition?

I choked a little. "Are you sure? I'm beyond honored. Thank you."

I called Jason and Jeff. "Your mom will be honored at a gala and will be receiving a pretty cool award. Will you guys escort me?"

Don Quixote Lifetime Achievement Award.

They agreed. As I prepared my acceptance speech, I asked God if this award was His way of erasing my doubts and restoring my confidence? His answer echoed clear. This award reflected the world's recognition. But God had already given me my true award when I stood on a stage of sorrow as His promises reminded me:

I have summoned you by name; you are mine. When you pass through the waters, I will be with you; and when you pass through the rivers, they will not sweep over you. When you walk through the fire, you will not be burned; the flames will not set you ablaze. For I am the Lord, your God, the Holy One of Israel, your Savior. (Isaiah 43:1-3)

With overwhelming gratitude, I lifted my inner voice in praise. *Heavenly Father, what a delightful reminder that I am Yours and You are my God and Savior. What greater award could I ever want? You kept me from drowning in the river of pain. You shielded me from burning in the fire of heartache.*

God used another Bible passage to remind me that I wasn't the only one called to a time-out of difficult trials and patient waiting. After slaying Goliath and being anointed as the next king of Israel, David had endured many long years of waiting and exile before he actually ascended the throne. The words King David wrote describing that time were equally true in my own life.

I waited patiently for the LORD to help me, and he turned to me and heard my cry. He lifted me out of the pit of despair, out of the mud and the mire. He set my feet on solid ground and steadied me as I walked along. He has given me a new song to sing, a hymn of praise to our God. Many will see what he has done and be amazed. They will put their trust in the LORD. (Psalm 40:1-3)

Here too was God's clear answer to my dilemma. *Many will be amazed by what God has done! They will put their trust in the*

LORD! All God asked of me was to lift my hymn of praise for what He'd done in my life. As I pointed my listeners to God's amazing deeds, they would see Him, not me. They would be drawn to God's faithfulness and put their trust in Him, not be sidetracked by any ugliness that stained my own journey.

On the promises in these two passages, I declared my victory that very night. God hadn't kept me from drowning without a purpose. He hadn't shielded me from the fire of heartache without a reason. And He hadn't lifted me from the mud and mire of the pit of despair and set my feet on solid ground without a defined plan. God's plan was for me to move forward, not as a victim covered with scars but a victor displaying the splendor of His restoring power.

I placed that precious award in the glass case of my heart as an ever-present remembrance of how God had walked me out of the pit of despair. Then I called the pastor of our new church home. "I'd be honored and truly blessed to speak at all four services."

"Including the Spanish one?"

I chuckled. "*Sí.*"

But after delivering my message, God had another surprise that would change my life.

Chapter Thirty-Two
New Beginning

You meant evil against me, but God meant it for good.

—Genesis 50:20

My hands were sweaty and my mouth dry as I stood at the pulpit of our new church. There was no going back. I'd made the commitment to speak at all four services. But standing in front of an audience after my life had been turned upside-down was like crossing a busy street without my white cane.

The moment I took the microphone in my hand, I felt the presence of the Holy Spirit in my heart. Doubt fled, and courage flooded back into me as I began sharing passionately what Christ had done for me, through me, and in spite of me. As always, I began my presentation with humor. The congregation laughed, and we bonded.

*Janet's return to the platform to share
her testimony of victory.*

With fresh confidence, I settled into the speaker role for which
God had molded me. I addressed my words to every heart in the
audience sinking in the bitterness of sorrow, shaken by betrayal or

failure, grappling with painfully unwanted transitions. Illustrations from my own life made clear my listeners didn't have to be blind to see God's purpose in their own lives. They didn't have to be defeated by injustice. Nor did they have to live battered by life's circumstances. Instead, they could each be conquerors because of God's power to overcome all their troubles.

With renewed boldness, I stated the battle between the evil of this world and the goodness of God. On the one side, Satan schemes to harm us, rob us of peace, erase our hope, and continue his viciousness into our future. But because of the Holy Spirit's power at work in us, Satan will ultimately be crushed and his schemes dismantled. God's triumph over all evil will usher in majestic victory, the radiance of success, and inexplicable joy. And God's plans for us are not just for eternity, but to offer us a hope and future today as He promised through the prophet Jeremiah.

> "For I know the plans I have for you," declares the LORD, "plans to prosper you and not to harm you, plans to give you hope and a future."
>
> —Jeremiah 29:11

I went on to chronicle for my listeners how the bitter journey of my life had been dotted with the sweetness of God's grace. I listed the lies of the world but also showed the promises of God. I detailed each stage that threatened to sink me and how I was lifted by God's strong arm instead. Every moment of grief God had replaced with comforting peace.

The best part of that day was the many listeners who shared of being amazed and drawn to God by my message. After each service, a lovely church member helped me off the stage and down the aisle to a display table where my books had been set up. As I stood beside the display, one person after another approached to express how my message had touched them and that my story of triumph had helped them see their own life troubles differently.

After the third service, one man with a charming voice shook my hand and introduced himself. "My name is Dale. Thank you so much for your message. I've been battling the loss of my wife for over two years. Now I'm inspired to go on."

I gave him a hug as was my custom with each person who approached. "What a blessing to hear that. Thank you for sharing."

The following Sunday, Mom and I were back to our usual church routine. But unlike previous Sundays, most of the congregation now knew me as well as the details of my story. One Sunday, Dale greeted Mom and me. "I've got a question for you. How long have you been attending this church?"

"For about six months."

He gasped. "That's hard to believe. As head usher, I'm usually standing here at the door every service. How is it I never noticed you or your mom come in or leave before?"

"Maybe you have a vision problem too?" I suggested. We both laughed.

After that, Mom and I stopped to chat with Dale each time we walked out of church. One day, a rental property Mom owned needed some work. I'd learned that one of Dale's many skills, was doing house repairs, so I emailed him for advice. He immediately replied with a recommendation of someone he knew with expertise in that area. His response was the beginning of a series of friendly emails and eventually phone calls.

As with many who connect with me, my hope was always to impart comfort in their grieving process. As we chatted on the phone, Dale shared further about his life and how he was dealing with the loss of his wife. The more we talked, the more apparent it became that our views, goals, values, and desires to further God's Kingdom aligned with each other. I grew to admire Dale's devotion to Christ and commitment to honor Him by serving others.

My own passion continued to be honoring my Lord by imparting more messages of God's great faithfulness. After my year-long hiatus, I was once again accepting additional speaking invitations.

As the weeks went by, Mom and I settled into our new normal. But that normal was about to change.

Dale and I had continued to chat occasionally by phone as well as at church. Then one day he invited me out to dinner. Gulp! Calling a close friend, I told her about the invitation. "It's a crazy thing. But there's no way at my age and in my situation I should accept an invitation from a man to dinner."

"Get a life, girlfriend!" my friend responded, much to my surprise. "What's wrong with you? If God put this friend in your path, what's wrong with having dinner with him?"

That night I journaled:

Lord, could this really be from You? I asked You for three things. To allow me to continue in ministry. To help me take care of Mom. And to guard me from loneliness. You have very clearly answered the first two. Is it possible that You are answering my third request with this invitation? I just need to know You are the one opening this door. So, I pray in complete trust that You will block this path if it's not from You or doesn't align with Your plans for my life. I will take each step forward until I see Your hand stopping me.

Throughout my years of ministry, I'd gone to numerous foreign countries alone. I'd encountered many adventures in unknown places. But this new venture with Dale carried new apprehensions. Greeting each other on Sundays and chatting occasionally on the phone was one thing. Spending time with him socially stirred up a tad of uneasiness. After much prayer for courage and wisdom, I stepped into that foreign terrain, fully confident God would protect me and block my path if this wasn't His will.

But instead of stopping me, God ushered me forward. We had a good time on that first dinner date. Wrapped in a gift box of gladness, romance soon painted our relationship. Eventually, Dale mentioned marriage. I gasped inside. I hadn't even been alone for a full two years. Was this too soon for such a momentous lifetime decision?

Returning to my normal default any time I was in doubt, I went to God in prayer. *Lord, I'm not sure how to respond here. Please grant me clarity in my thinking and more wisdom to know Your will.*

Just then the story of Abigail in 1 Samuel 25 popped in my head. Married to an abusive drunkard, Abigail's decisive nature when her husband's wickedness led to a showdown with David, saved her household, and also prevented David from wrongdoing. Shortly after, God struck Abigail's husband down for his evil behavior, and David immediately proposed marriage. The Bible account made clear that Abigail's unusual encounter and subsequent marriage to David was no coincidence but God's divine plan for Abigail's life. Which gave me a biblical pattern for my own response.

While I'd been praying for guidance, I'd accepted an invitation to speak in Ecuador. During my time there, Dale visited my mom to seek her blessing should we choose to marry. His kind, attentive nature made it easy for Mom to bond with him. She giggled like a little girl each time he came to the door. When he told her of his desire to marry me, she sighed with delight and gave her blessing.

My sons were a different story. Jason questioned Dale astutely. "I have to know how you feel about my mom's blindness. Are you willing to deal with that?"

"Your mom sees better than any of us," Dale responded.

Jeff expressed even stronger concern. He wasn't sure if Dale would take care of me, and he was hesitant about his mom being in a relatively new situation with a man he didn't know. But once Dale and Jeff spent some time in conversation, Jeff accepted our relationship. Dale's grown children did the same.

When I came back from Ecuador, Dale proposed. I accepted. I also invited God's continued involvement as we entered into this unexpected season, leaning on the Holy Spirit to be by my side.

Pleasant moments filled that season. Mom, Dale, and I developed a routine after Sunday service. We would head to our favorite restaurant, then spend Sunday afternoons together at my house. While Dale listened intently, Mom told stories of our life in Bolivia, our journey to this country, and her passion to know Jesus.

One morning when I entered the kitchen, Mom pulled out a stool at the kitchen island. "Sit over here."

I knew this meant she wanted to share something important with me. Sometimes she gave me a motherly scolding that I was working too many hours and not getting enough rest. This time her tone was more serious than usual. "I know I've told you this before, Janet, but I don't want you to forget. Everything for my cremation is in order and has been paid for. I showed you where the paperwork is in the closet, right?"

"Yes, Mom, you've told me that repeatedly. You even told Dale, remember?" Reaching to give her a hug, I added teasingly, "In any case, where do you think you're going? After all, how many ninety-two-year-old ladies enjoy the perfect health you do?"

"Ninety-two and a half," she corrected me in a sing-song tone.

"You're right. And at that age, you don't take any medications at all. Your mind is more alert than the rest of us, and your contagious joy never ends." I shook my head. "So, no more talk about cremation or any of that stuff."

Taking my hand in her own tiny one, she said in a tone as loving and gentle as a dove's coo, "No, no don't think that way. We're not meant to live here forever. This isn't our home. Heaven is our permanent home. That's where I look forward to living with Jesus forever."

The new beginning.

Dale and I also looked forward to a special event, our wedding day. Standing at the altar in the church where we'd met, we pronounced our vows before God, family, and friends. As we did so, gratitude flooded our hearts for the way God had brought restoration to our pain, reassurance for our days, and hope for our future.

Once back from our honeymoon, the daily routine of our married life always included Mom. We enjoyed an afternoon snack together, watching *Andy Griffith* on TV, attending church as a threesome each Sunday. Then just eighteen months later, COVID attacked me. I recovered, but Mom became ill as well. Pneumonia compromised her breathing, and she had to be hospitalized. Two weeks later, we brought her home. With the family around her, she slipped like a precious angel into the splendor of her permanent heavenly home.

At Mom's memorial service, we celebrated her life, not her loss. She hadn't died but had simply left the land of the dying for the land of the living. The joy of the Lord had always overflowed and been her strength wherever her tiny frame went, and it would be ours too.

Mom was probably smiling from heaven when I received an invitation to enter the 2022 Ms. Senior Florida Pageant. At first, I dismissed the idea with a chuckle. A beauty pageant seemed frivolous at best. But the pageant director insisted and offered me a scholarship that waived the entry fee.

I accepted with some remaining hesitation. But once I'd signed the contract, I gave it my all, aware I was this pageant's very first blind contestant. I prepared my philosophy of life, shopped for my evening gown, and prepared for the judges' interview. For the talent competition, I practiced and practiced the flamenco/salsa dance.

Dancing was the easy part. Finding a way to face the audience as I turned and twirled was a challenge. Unable to see, I could have ended up with my back to them. But by then I knew to trust in God's faithfulness, which always shines even in the smallest details.

This time was no different. Dale and I came up with a solution, which was to place a small carpet on the floor for me to feel with my feet as a reference point. It worked. I welcomed the challenge and enjoyed the experience. I received awards for the best philosophy of life and best judge's interview. And what fun to hear my family cheer when I was named first runner-up for the title of Ms. Senior Florida 2022!

First Runner-Up, 2022 Ms. Senior Florida Pageant.

Best Philosophy of Life Award,
Ms. Senior Florida Pageant, 2022.

Best Judge's Interview,
Ms. Senior Florida Pageant, 2022.

But a more valuable prize came a few months later when Jeff and his wife Krystal brought into our life a sweet little baby.

As I held her two-day-old tiny body in my arms,

I ran my fingertips across her velvet cheeks. I inhaled the aroma of God's love. I sensed the beauty of a new life. The beginning of fresh hope. The dawning of sweet expectations, renewed joy, and God's promise of new tomorrows. My next journal entry reads:

Lord, among the roses of blessings in the garden of my life, thorns have made my heart bleed. Yet the downpour of your grace has washed my wounds clean, dried my every tear, and wiped away all my fears. With new vision, I see the color of gratitude and hope that paints the landscape of my life.

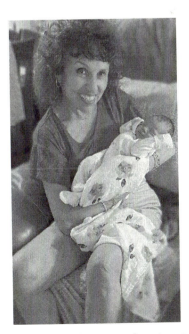

Newborn grandbaby, new beginning of life.

Jason, wife Rachel, and children Alyssa and Kamden.

Jeff, wife Krystal, and baby Eliana.

Epilogue
Not the End

In the introduction of this book, I invited you, dear reader and friend, into the privacy of my journey. Thank you for accepting my invitation. How beautiful that you have joined me in the storms of my life that God has turned to calm seas.

Now it is your turn. Your own deliciously wonderful new beginning. Before you turn the last page and dash off to your life, I want you to know that Jesus is in the midst of writing your story too. But there may be a pause. That's because Jesus doesn't barge uninvited into our lives. He waits for us to invite Him in.

If you haven't done so yet, Jesus is waiting for that invitation. He has the map for your journey already traced, the turns marked, the stops defined, and the destination identified as beautifully triumphant. No matter where you are right now in life, how big the mess, how dark the sin, how deep the shame or sorry mistakes,

Jesus is ready to pour out His living water to wash away those stains, mend your wounds, and erase the scars. With His amazing grace and unfailing love that is always with you, your vibrant new journey will lead you to a wonderful horizon of victorious episodes.

And now it's about time to turn that last page. But even though this book is finished, I hope and pray, dear reader, that our friendship has just began. I'm still here for you. Need guidance in your new life with Jesus? Have questions about the story? Need explanations? Or maybe you just need to talk or share your own life journey. Whatever it is, I'm delighted to connect with you. You can just drop me a note at janet@janetperezeckles.com.

For more information including my other books, videos, blog posts, and more, go to www.janetperezeckles.com.

ABOUT THE AUTHOR

Blindness hasn't stopped Janet Perez Eckles from becoming an author of five inspirational books, an international speaker, radio host, and Founder of JC Empowerment Ministries. Her writings have appeared in thirty-two *Chicken Soup for the Soul* titles, and hundreds of print and online publications. She has been featured on Christian radio and TV programs from Focus on the Family to the 700 Club and on the cover of Hispanic Woman Magazine. Janet lives in Florida with husband Dale, adult children, and delightful grandchildren.

She can be contacted at: www.janetperezeckles.com.

DID YOU ENJOY THIS BOOK?

Dear Reader,

Your feedback means the world to me. May I ask you to jot a few lines as a review and post it wherever you got your copy of my book? This way you and I can spread the word and encourage those who are hurting.

Thank you!

Much Love,

Janet

Made in the USA
Columbia, SC
29 April 2023

15649884R00164